THE UNIVERSITY OF
WINCHESTER

Martial Rose Library
Tel: 01962 827306

To be returned on or before the day marked above, subject to recall.

MANCHESTER

The political philosophy of Jean-Jacques Rousseau

The impossibility of reason

Mads Qvortrup

Manchester University Press

Manchester and New York

distributed exclusively in the USA by Palgrave

The right of Mads Qvortrup to be identified as the author of this work has been asserted by him in accordance with the Copyright, Designs and Patents Act 1988.

Published by Manchester University Press
Oxford Road, Manchester M13 9NR, UK
and Room 400, 175 Fifth Avenue, New York, NY 10010, USA
www.manchesteruniversitypress.co.uk

Distributed exclusively in the USA by
Palgrave, 175 Fifth Avenue, New York,
NY 10010, USA

Distributed exclusively in Canada by
UBC Press, University of British Columbia, 2029 West Mall,
Vancouver, BC, Canada V6T 1Z2

British Library Cataloguing-in-Publication Data
A catalogue record for this book is available from the British Library

Library of Congress Cataloging-in-Publication Data applied for

ISBN   0 7190 6580 1 *hardback*
           0 7190 6581 X *paperback*

First published 2003

11 10 09 08 07 06 05 04 03   10 9 8 7 6 5 4 3 2 1

Typeset by Freelance Publishing Services, Brinscall, Lancs
www.freelancepublishingservices.co.uk
Printed in Great Britain
by Bell and Bain Ltd, Glasgow

Durate et vosmet rebus servate secundis
(Endure, and keep yourselves for days of happiness)
Virgil, *Aenied*, I, 205

Contents

Preface

There is a story behind every book. This one is no exception. Whilst a graduate student I worked on a doctorate on the practical impossibility of direct democracy. For rhetorical purposes I wanted to use Rousseau as a philosophical straw-man – i.e. as someone who defended the position I sought to reject. I browsed through the *Discourse on Inequality* and *Du Contrat Social* in search for incriminating quotes but found to my surprise (and subsequent delight) that my misgivings about the Genevan thinker had been both ill-informed and wrong. He did not conform to the stereotype as a native participationist, indeed he expressed the very same misgivings about direct democracy that I had reached. In short; Rousseau was closer to Montesquieu than to Robespierre. What I also found was that he had views about social cohesion, European integration (he was against), nationalism (he advocated it), free-trade (he opposed it), sustainable development (he promoted it), and secularism (he lamented it). In other words he took a stand on many of the issues that shape the political debate at the time of writing. This in itself, I found, made him worth studying.

This book seeks to: present an overview of Rousseau's political philosophy and its relation to his general philosophy (his philosophical development, an introduction to his main ideas on philosophy, religion, morality and education); place Rousseau's thought in the context of different traditions in the history of West European thought; show that Rousseau's political thinking was based on a profound (conservative) scepticism, which caused him to embrace institutional mechanisms that could prevent legislation; demonstrate that he shared Burke's opposition to revolutionary change; show that he developed an early case for a nationalist ideology, which could perform the functions of civic religion.

The book does not seek to end all discussion – it rather seeks the opposite; to begin a serious discussion of politics based on the insights of one of the foremost of the classics. All too often philosophy is becoming detached from everyday life. It is my hope that this book will show that philosophy can also be a practical discipline. As another great master, Karl Marx, once said: 'The philosophers have merely interpreted the world differently. The point, however, is to change it' (Marx 1983: 7). This book seeks to show that Rousseau's political philosophy can make a positive contribution to this 'change' – though not in a way that Marx would have approved of.

The book is divided into five chapters. Chapter 1 presents an overview of Rousseau's life and times. More than any other writer Rousseau's philosophy has – rightly or wrongly – been associated with his life (as outlined in his many autobiographies). There is something to be said for this interpretation. Without an understanding of his life it is difficult to appreciate why he wrote the works he wrote, and what he sought to accomplish. Yet his biographers have often presented an incomplete account of his life, one based only on his own autobiographical writings. In Chapter 1 this tendency is challenged by using Rousseau's letters and eyewitness accounts by comtempories *as well as* his autobiographical writings to paint a more nuanced picture of the Swiss philosopher. Chapter 1 also presents the range of Rousseau's genius, which included operas, plays, novels, as well as political, economic, botanical and theological writings. Rousseau's work is related to the geniuses who were inspired by his writings, such as Goethe, Kant and John F. Kennedy.

In Chapter 2 we outline the major philosophical problem for Rousseau: the burden of modernity. An account is given of Rousseau's place in the emerging world of modernity, and his opposition to secularism and scientism. It is shown how his general philosophical – and theological – opposition to modernity underpinned his moral philosophy. Unlike liberal, or utilitarian, thinkers (I use the term interchangeably) – Rousseau sought to base his moral judgements on emotions and sensibility, *not* on rational calculations. It is shown how this made him overcome the poverty of ethical theory that has characterised modernity – and how Rousseau invented post-modernism (with a pre-modern face). Chapter 2 also contains a section on Rousseau's economic philosophy, in which it is shown that he – like Adam Smith – succeeded in transcending the economic theories of mercantilists and physiocrats. Yet Rousseau's solution pointed in a direction that differed from that of his Scottish contemporary, especially in attacking free trade and defending a system of sustainable growth – including an awareness of environmental issues. Chapter 2 further presents an analysis of the relationship between Rousseau and Burke. Often seen as adversaries, the chapter shows – and proves with extensive quotes – that Rousseau and Burke, in fact, were in agreement on the majority of issues, including opposition to revolutionary change, reverence for religion and a preference for gradual reform.

Chapter 3 likewise breaks with traditional scholarship (or rather the lack of it!). Often presented as a proto-totalitarian, Rousseau has traditionally been seen as an opponent of constitutionalism, checks and balances, and the separation of powers (Talmon 1952; Riker 1981). Following a brief history of the history of constitutionalism (from Moses to the French Revolution), Rousseau's political writings are compared with the writings of constitutionalists like James Madison and Baron de Montesquieu. It is shown that Rousseau shared the view that checks and balances are necessary for preventing the corruption of power and that he advocated a system of the separation of powers (and spoke highly of the British constitution. Yet, contrary to the other constitutionalists, Rousseau was a democrat. Whereas Montesquieu and Madison wanted the elites to check the elites (through the introduction of second chambers and constitutional courts), Rousseau emphasised that the executive ought to be checked by the people. He thus anticipated the political system that was instated by the American populists (including Theodore Roosevelt and Woodrow Wilson). However, unlike other constitutionalists, Rousseau did not believe that institutions themselves would be sufficient for creating a good polity. He ceaselessly emphasised that political education was necessary for creating a good society. An understanding of his constitutionalism is not enough – as Fralin (1974) seems to contend. Rather it is necessary to read his institutional writings in connection with his educational writings, and as a part of the same overall project (something Charvet (1974) also has emphasised).

This latter theme is continued in Chapter 4. Previously unrecognised by scholars of nationalism, Rousseau was, in fact, the founder of the modern doctrine of nationalism (arguably the most successful of all the modern ideologies). It is shown how Rousseau succeeded in developing a case for social cohesion and the necessity of having a common culture in a society. In developing a case for nationalism as a 'civic profession of faith' he continued – and redeveloped – a doctrine begun by Machiavelli, which was later to be further elaborated by Alexis de Tocqueville and present-day theorists and practitioners of *social capital*, like the political scientist Robert Putnam and the English politician David Blunkett. It is argued that Rousseau accomplished the feat of developing a new doctrine of civic religion (i.e. nationalism) and that he – unlike Machiavelli –

succeeded in combining a defence for this doctrine with a new place for Christianity (which was consistent with the original apolitical teachings of Christ). Chapter 4 also presents an account of Rousseau's thinking on international politics – including something as timely as an account of his opposition against the establishment of a European superstate.

Chapter 5 presents the conclusions, and shows that there was an internal coherence in Rousseau's thought. Chapter 6 rounds off this *tour de force* of Rousseau's political philosophy by an account of his philosophy of music, which can be seen as a metaphor for his general philosophy.

Acknowledgements

Needless to say this book could not have been written without the generous help support and encouragement of a number of people (although the usual caveat applies!). I am indebted to David Miller, Oxford, for pointing me to Rousseau's nationalist writings, to Jürgen Habermas for curing my contextualist delusions – and for doing so in a way that shows that he practices what he preaches. I am further indebted to the late Robert Nozick for teaching me that a political thinker should always be ready to radically revise initial conceptions. I also wish to thank John Grey, Brendan O'Leary, Erik Ringmar, Ethan Putterman, John Charvet, George Tsebelis, Kenneth Minogue, Gordon Smith, Alex Cambridge, Sascha Qvortrup, Steffen Qvortrup, Tracey Gafoor, David Blunkett, Nina Hilfensohn, Fergal McDonnell, Ed Page, Thomas Konig, Gary Sussman, George Jones, Ernest Thorpe, John Parillo-Hess, the two anonymous referees – and my editors Tony Mason and Richard Delahunty. Lastly I am grateful to Pia, Sebastian and Frederik for letting me work on this book when I really should have spent more time in the playground.

Mads Qvortrup, Oxford

Introduction and method

Great star what was thy happiness if thou shineth for no one? (Friedrich
Nietzsche, 1888: 5)[1]

'Today is Freedom day' thundered the headline in the *Independent*, a British
newspaper, on 1 May 1997. The perplexing headline was followed by a no
less mystifying quote: 'The English people believes itself to be free: it is
gravely mistaken; it is free only during the election of MPs; as soon as the
Members are elected the members are enslaved.' The quote was followed
by the name J-.J. Rousseau. On the day when the Labour Party was about
to win a landslide victory over then Prime Minister John Major's accident-
prone administration, a national newspaper chose to cite a long deceased
philosopher, and not to probe into the incoming government's proposed
policies, or the outgoing administration's (dismal) record. A strange
editorial decision perhaps, but an interesting one all the same. The
Independent's decision to quote Rousseau on the front page, on the day of
the most important election for a generation, shows that classical
philosophers are taken seriously, and is indicative of the underlying (tacit)
assumption that Rousseau has something to say to us even today, more
than two hundred years after his death. This is a book about Rousseau,
which outlines his philosophy, precisely because he – the most untimely
of all the great minds – somehow diagnosed the state of our society before
it was formed or fully established. This might sound mystifying, yet it is
not an altogether radical position. Indeed, most of the tradition of Western
philosophy has been based on the assumption that philosophy (as opposed
to science) reveals timeless truths. For this reason it is necessary that each
generation seeks to establish contact with the living thoughts of deceased
men and women. Machiavelli – another thinker in the premier league of
great minds – once wrote about this (after he had fallen from grace and
was exiled from his country):

> When evening has come, I return to my house and go into my study. At the
> door I take off my clothes of the day, covered with mud and mire, and I put
> on my regal and courtly garments; and decently re-clothed, I enter the an-
> cient courts of ancient men, where, received by them lovingly, I feed on the
> food that alone is mine and that I was born for. There I am not ashamed to
> speak with them and to ask them the reason for their actions; and they in
> their humanity reply to me. And for the space of four hours I feel no
> boredom, I forget every pain, I do not fear poverty, death does not frighten
> me. I deliver myself entirely to them. (Machiavelli 1994: 3)

Two hundred years later, one of his most famous disciples, Jean-Jacques
Rousseau, sought to emulate the Florentine master, by taking up his pen.
Like his philosopher colleague, the Swiss thinker also believed that political
philosophy should be a continuing dialogue with the classics. In the
introduction to the *Discourse sur l'inégalité* (*The Origin of Inequality*),
Rousseau, almost echoing Machiavelli, set out to transcend history and
speak directly to all of mankind.

> As my subject of interest is mankind in general, I shall endeavour to make use
> of a style adapted to all nations, or rather forgetting time and place, to attend
> only to men to whom I am speaking. I shall suppose myself in the Lyceum of
> Athens, repeating the lessons of my masters, with Plato and Socrates for my
> judges, and the whole of the human race for audience. (III: 135)

This little book is an attempt to re-open a dialogue with the classics. It
attempts not only to see the masters in context – as has become popular
among modern thinkers – but rather to seek inspiration from the great
minds to deal with contemporary political problems. Rousseau – and
indeed any other classic – is politically relevant *only* if he reveals timeless
insights. If a classic cannot inspire he is nothing, and is better confined to
the dustbin of failed political doctrines.

This book is based on the premise – to be supported in the text – that
Rousseau *speaks through the ages*. It seeks to show that Rousseau, while he
may not have the answers to contemporary problems, at the very least
provides new angles and perspectives on the debate. By failing to take
these contributions seriously we rob ourselves of an important source of
inspiration when we deal with the political problems of our times. Of
course, Rousseau is not the only thinker to inspire. Marx, Plato, Smith,
Aristotle, Madison, Hobbes, Hegel and Locke have made other – in many
ways equally interesting and valuable – contributions to that never-ending
debate which is political philosophy. This book, however, presents a
perspective from the point of view of Rousseau. It is to be hoped that
others will take up the challenge, and translate the doctrines of the other

great minds into contemporary politics. For the classics are not merely dinosaurs who stalk the academic scene, apparently impervious to the natural selection of so-called scientific progress; rather they avail themselves for discussions with posterity – a discussion that will never be concluded.

To follow this approach is likely to attract criticism. The bulk of British writers on the subject of the history of ideas follow a contextual approach (Skinner 1969). Quintin Skinner – the foremost of the contextutalists – has rejected the idea that the classics may have political relevance beyond their own time. He has gone so far as saying that it 'must be a mistake even to try to write intellectual biographies concentrating on the works of a given writer, or to write histories of ideas tracing the morphology of a given concept over time' (Skinner 1969: 48). For, as he goes on, 'the classic texts are concerned with their own alien problems' (52). Any 'statement is inescapably the embodiment of particular intentions, or a particular occassion', and thus specific to its context in a way that it can only be 'naïve to try to transcend' (50).

Skinner has a point. Rousseau was obviously a product of his age. As is natural, even for a genius, he reacted to developments in his own age. Yet this does not mean that we cannot learn from his writings. Moreover, in addition to explicitly stating that he was writing for all subsequent generations (see above), Rousseau arguably wrote about issues that were as salient then as they are now. The issue that 'power corrupts' may serve as an illustration.

Rulers have always sought absolute power (or as few restraints as possible), hence the nature of the problem of constitutionalism has stayed unaltered, although the political circumstances have changed. It is, of course, true that we – as readers – belong to different traditions, and all reading is a dialogue with the author. We come to the classic text from within our personal hermeneutic horizons, which colour our reading. Yet this does not mean that we cannot learn from the classic. As German philosopher Hans-Georg Gadamer puts it (Gadamer 1960: 184), our 'pre-conception' (*Vorurteile*) may colour our reading but the process goes both ways, and in the process of reading, our own 'hermeneutic horizon' changes as a result of our reading. By engaging with the text we modify our prejudices –and broaden our horizon. It is the latter part of the 'Hermeneutic circle' (356) which is the stuff of a practical and applied reading of the classics of Western philosophy.

Reading the classics is more than just overcoming the hermeneutical problems of reading prose from a bygone age. The classical masters were broad thinkers, and as such they inspired many different interpretations from a wide range of diverse – and often unrelated – academic subjects. Rousseau is no exception to this. As Judith Shklar has noted, 'even among his versatile contemporaries he was extraordinary: composer, musicologist, playwright, drama critic, novelist, botanist, pedagogue, political philosopher, psychologist' (Shklar 1970: 5). Being primarily a work of political philosophy the question is: how much of this is relevant for the political theorist? Indeed which texts, published or unpublished, paint a true picture of what he *really* meant? Ought we to include everything that Rousseau ever wrote? And, if not, where do we draw the line? What qualifies as Rousseau's political writings? This is far from being a trivial question. As Michel Foucault observed (when writing about a related subject in 'What is an Author?'):

> Even when an individual has been accepted as an author, we must still ask if everything that he wrote, said, or left behind is part of his work. The problem is both theoretical and technical. When undertaking the publication of Nietzsche's works, for example, where should one stop? (Foucault 1996a: 106)

Foucault believed it impossible to draw the line – he even mused that we had to consider the shopping list as a part of the collected works! Foucault notwithstanding, this study has (for practical purposes) included primarily Rousseau's political writings (Volume III of his *Collected Works* in the Pléiade edition), secondarily his letters and non-political writings (e.g. his writings on music, poetry and botany), and accounts by contemporary authors. By including everything that Rousseau wrote for publication and his letters we base the study on the assumption that there is an internal coherence in his thought, which is reflected in his remarks about politics throughout his oeuvre. The hypothesis is that an understanding of his political philosophy is deepened by an understanding of his so-called non-political works. This view is not universally accepted (Skinner 1969: 52).

Rather than focusing on the whole oeuvre, writers have concentrated on smaller parts of his output, with the result that critics 'have collaborated in producing the mirage of two [or even more] Rousseaus' (Kavanagh 2001: 397). Thus there is one Rousseau

> for political scientists and historians of philosophy, another for students of literature and psychology. As inevitable as that border may appear, it has led to a fragmentation that can compromise our understanding of his work. The real challenge in reading Rousseau is to appreciate how his political vision depends on his literary and autobiographical writings while at the

same time recognising the extend to which his literary representations of subjectivity flow from a dialectic of self and other at the core of his political writings. (Kavanagh 2001: 397)

This study is an attempt to do exactly this – and to do so in a way that makes Rousseau a participant in the political debates of the present day. As a discussion partner – rather than as a prophet – we should not accept the words of the ancient masters of yesteryear uncritically. Rousseau would have concurred with the latter view. As he wrote in a letter to Usteri (a Genevan preacher):

> My dear friend, I do not propose to convince you. I know that no two heads are organised alike, and that after a good many disputations, a good many objections, a good many clarifications, everyone always ends up adhering to the same sentiments as before … I may have been mistaken always. I have undoubtedly been mistaken often. I have stated my reasons it is up to the public, it is up to you to weigh them, to judge, to choose. (*Lettre à Usteri*, 1763, *Collected Works* XVII: 62–5)

Notes

1 '*Du grosses Gestirn! Was wäre dein Glück Wenn du nicht die hättest, welchen du leuchtest?*' Friedrich Nietzsche, *Also Sprach Zaratrustra. Ein Buch für Alle und Keinen* (Chemnitz: Verlag von Ernest Schmeitzner, 1888), p. 5.

1

The politics of the soul:
the life and times of Jean-Jacques Rousseau[1]

For what is a man profited, if he shall gain the whole world, and lose his own soul? (St Matthew, 16.26)

Did Ludwig Wittgenstein write the most successful love story of his century? Did Thomas Hobbes compose an opera – and did it inspire the work of Mozart? Did Byron write poems about Hume or Leibniz? Did Schiller compose sonnets about Descartes and Locke? These questions seem too ridiculous to warrant an answer. Ask the same questions about Jean-Jacques Rousseau (1712–78) and the opposite is true. The composer of *Le devin du village* (the favourite opera of Louis XV), the author of *La Nouvelle Héloïse* (the best-selling novel in the eighteenth century), Rousseau was more than the famed educationalist and the 'author of the French revolution'. He inspired Mozart, Derrida, Tolstoi, Kant, Marie Antoinette, Emile Durkheim, Byron, Goethe and Simone Weil, as well as politicians like Maximilien Robespierre, Thomas Jefferson, Simon de Bolivar and John F. Kennedy.

It is not surprising that this literary genius continues to fascinate.[2] 'A classic', noted T.S. Eliot, 'is someone who establishes a culture' (Eliot 1975: 402). Few others than Plato, Virgil and Christ (and the latter, arguably, had unfair parental support!) can lay claim to this status. As one scholar has put it, 'In our time Rousseau is usually cited as a classic of early modern political philosophy. He is more than that: he is the central figure in the history of modern philosophy and perhaps the pivotal figure in modern culture as a whole' (Velkley 2002: 31). Rousseau belongs to the noble few. Reviled and ridiculed, liked or loathed, the Swiss vagabond, who never attended university, let alone owned land or held privileges is, perhaps, alongside Karl Marx, the only modern thinker who qualifies as a 'classic'.

Rousseau was aware of his genius but not unaware of his humble beginnings. 'Never forget', he wrote, 'that he who is speaking is neither a philosopher, nor a scholar, but a simple man, a man of truth, unprejudiced, without a system' (Rousseau in Riley 2001: 12). But he was also a sensitive – if occasionally paranoid – man, who penned the most penetrating, revealing, and at times, pathetic autobiography in the history of Western literature, namely *Les Confessions*. Having antagonised his former friends among the *Encycloplédistes*, the Genevan authorities, the Catholic Church, and just about everyone else, Rousseau did himself few favours by writing his *Confessions* – and his other autobiographical writings, *Dialouges: Rousseau juge de Jean-Jacques* (1776), *Les rêveries du promeneur solitaire* (1778), and his letters to the French censor Malesherbes in 1762. As Byron noted about Rousseau, in *Childe Harold's Pilgrimage*: 'His life was one long war with self-sought foes' (Byron 1994: 214).

He had wanted to defend himself against the authorities, and against the accusations levied against his educational tract, *Emile ou de L'education* (1762). To this effect he wrote, albeit unsuccessfully, *Lettres écrites de la montagne* (1764), which made matters worse. Increasingly paranoid, he turned to his *apologiae*; his autobiographical writings. How many pages does it take to write *mea culpa*? Rousseau didn't seem to know.

It cannot be denied that Rousseau created art out of his sufferings, nor that these writings themselves contain elements of a profound political philosophy. Yet not everybody has been convinced. Paul de Man, the American literary critic, found that 'the more there is to expose the more there is to be ashamed of; the more resistance to exposure the more satisfying the scene' (De Man 1979: 285). Perhaps. But there is also another interpretation. Namely that Rousseau's philosophy is based on the assertion that man is naturally good and has been corrupted by society. This was metaphorically reflected in his autobiographical writings, argues a perceptive scholar:

> The picture of Jean-Jacques's departure from and return to nature is a part of the moral fable of the *Confessions* as well as a complementary part of Rousseau's system. With the account of his own life, Rousseau gives a persuasive image of human experience. Jean-Jacques may be too idiosyncratic and at times too unattractive to be an exemplary figure. Nevertheless, the description of his experience does transform the readers of the confessions by exposing them to a new way of looking at life. (Kelly 1987: 248)

Perhaps so, however, the public perception of Rousseau was not softened as a result of his personal revelations of his misdeeds. Edmund Burke –

his staunchest and first major critic – wrote scornfully (in *Letter to a Member of the National Assembly*) that 'the insane Socrates of the National Assembly [Rousseau], was impelled to publish his mad confessions of his mad faults, and to attempt a new sort of glory' (Burke 1991: 512). Not exactly a ringing endorsement, nor indeed a correct assessment – but a view adopted by many.[3]

Why did Rousseau write this autobiography? What is the point of revealing one's faults to one's enemies? It seems that he – a man of letters – believed that he could alter the public's perception by explaining the background. He misjudged the public. To understand all is not always to forgive all. Perhaps he should have known better. It is certainly ironic that Rousseau, at calmer moments, let Julie utter that 'taking so much trouble to justify oneself sometimes produces the contrary result' (Rousseau 1968, Letter XXXV from Julie). Maybe he should have heeded the advice of his fictional heroine.[4] He did not do this when he (ten years later) handed out notes to the Parisian citizens, complaining that France, 'once kind and affectionate', had 'changed towards an unfortunate foreigner who is alone and without support and defender' (I: 998).

It is hard not to resort to adjectives such as pathetic, mad or loony when describing this behaviour. Of course, Rousseau was not always like this – not even at the darkest periods of his life. It is worth remembering that Rousseau, at the very same time when he handed out desperate notes, also composed the supremely analytical *Considérations sur la gouvernement de Pologne* (1771).

Who was the real Rousseau? What was he like? A complex individual to be sure. However, his contemporaries' assessments of him were remarkably similar, consistent and positive. Giacomo Casanova, who visited the philosopher in 1759, described him as 'a man who reasoned well, whose manner was simple and modest' (Casanova 1968: 223). David Hume concurred, finding him, 'mild and gentle and modest and good humoured' (Hume 1932: 527). These portraits complement the picture painted of him by Thomas Bentley. Recalling a discussion that touched upon subjects as diverse as the geological interpretation of fossils and the American declaration of independence, Bentley wrote:

> He is a musical instrument above the concert pitch, and therefore too elevated for the present state of society, and all his singularities and errors, as they are called, proceed from the delicacy of his sensations. I was so taken up by his intellect that I almost forgot how it was clothed, though I remember he has a small slender body, rather below the common size, that he has a thin palish face with delicate features, and that he has great deal of

expression in his eyes and countenance when he is either pleased or displeased, one of which he certainly is every moment; for nothing that he sees or hears or thinks of is indifferent to him. When nature was making this singular being, one could imagine she intended him for the air, but before she had finished his wings he eagerly sprung out of her hands, and his unfinished body sank down to the earth. (Bentley quoted in France 1979: 9)

Not all of his contemporaries agreed. Voltaire held him in utter contempt – on hearing the news of Rousseau's death he wrote that 'he ate like a devil, getting indigestion, he died like a dog' (Voltaire 1973: 181). And this was one of his milder remarks! Yet there is a remarkable consistency in the descriptions of him as a simple man who seemed to personify his philosophical ideals of a (romanticised) Sparta.

No introduction to philosophy is complete without a narrative of the life of Rousseau. The story – recently (and admirably) told by the late Maurice Cranston (Cranston 1983; 1997) – has become almost mythological, and is well known even to less than avid readers of the European Canon. The story of the watch-maker's son from Geneva who failed to return to his apprenticeship, when he found himself locked out of the city, and the tale of how he – a young man abandoned by his father[5] – was taken in by Mme de Warrens, who converted him to Catholicism (and then seduced him!), is often retold. All this has become part of the tapestry of Western *Kulturgeschichte*. So too have the misdeeds of the famous and progressive educationalist who abandoned his own children to an unknown fate.[6] As if this wasn't enough Rousseau also revealed to the world how he suffered from urinary retention (I: 361).

Rousseau was trained in music. The musical training provided him with a vocational skill. For like most of the great men of letters, Rousseau did not earn his living from teaching at a university. It was note-copying, not writing, that provided him with a (modest) income. In the years before he was catapulted to fame he was extremely strapped for cash. After leaving *Les Charmettes* (Mme de Warrens' chateau) he tried his luck as a teacher for Mably's unruly children (and wrote an early treatise on the subject). Working as a tutor for the aristocracy was not uncommon among philosophers (Hobbes and Locke both earned their living in this way). However Rousseau – the great educationalist – showed little aptitude for pedagogy in practice. Increasingly driven by ambition and an almost Hegelian thirst for recognition, he went to Paris to seek fortune and fame. He found neither. However, he was able to charm influential ladies, like Madame de Broglie, who helped him land a job as a secretary to de Montaigu, the French ambassador to Venice. Rousseau duly went to Italy, was captivated by the country, its language and its music, but humiliated by his boss – especially because of his birth as a commoner and a foreigner. The proud republican found it humiliating to be ill treated by people who owed their positions not to their talents, but to the good fortune of being born to aristocratic parents. Rousseau was embittered but did not resign to his fate. He resigned from the job – and turned his anger into political philosophy.

It is remarkable given his obsession with music that this is the least studied subject in the otherwise vast scholarly literature about him (Riley 2001: 329),[7] yet it is questionable if Rousseau would have enjoyed the same following – and vilification – had he remained but a musician. It is highly probable that Rousseau would have been – and remained – an obscure eighteenth-century composer had he not read the prize question of the Academy in Dijon in *Mercure de France*, asking 'if the re-establishment of the arts and the sciences have contributed to an improvement in the morals of man' ('*Si le rétablissement des sciences et des arts a contribué à épurer les mœurs*') (III: 1). Furthermore, it is probable that his erstwhile friends among the *Philosophes* failed to grasp what this *bon sauvage* was all about, and that they – had they known the true Rousseau – would have sought to strangle him at his literary birth.

Rousseau had read the prize question to Dennis Diderot – whom he visited in prison. It might seem odd that Rousseau – an individual with professed belief in God, the afterlife and salvation through Jesus Christ (IV: 955) – shared the company of thinkers who strongly opposed religion. It seems stranger still that it was Diderot, a materialist and supporter of the *Whig interpretation of history*, who urged Rousseau to pen his essay. Rousseau was a man of passion to an extend that it was difficult for his fellow philosophers to fathom. Unlike the *Encycloplédistes* he was not a man of compromises – Voltaire was perfectly willing to stay silent; Rousseau was not.

Diderot, so it might be conjectured, saw the Dijon prize essay as just another journalistic challenge – as a possible candidate for a deconstruction of the interpretation that the arts and sciences had benefited mankind. Diderot did not – and could not – sympathise with Rousseau's view, but saw the essay as good sport and a challenging game.[8] For Rousseau it was anything but a game. Modernity was an evil, indeed, *the* evil, which had disenchanted the world. It is worth considering this aspect in some detail, as Rousseau's discontent with modernity and secularism, perhaps more than anything else, was the cause that fired his passion.

If there is a core to Rousseau's oeuvre it would be his anti-modernism and his anti-rationalism. Philosophy – by which he meant the sciences –

had clouded the worldview of man and led to a despair and lack of meaning (a feeling which was later to be depicted as *Sickness unto Death* by
another anti-rationalist, Søren Kierkegaard).[9] 'Instead of removing my
doubts and curing my uncertainties [the philosophers and the scientists]
have shaken all my most assured beliefs concerning the questions most
important to me.' These ardent 'missionaries of atheism' (I: 1016) have
done nothing for mankind.[10] This feeling caused a sensation, and created
a new trend in literature and politics. The sentiment that science had
demystified the world – that the scientists had produced a worldview
devoid of meaning by killing the graceful God of the Gospels in blind
pursuit of wanton mathematical truths – was a central element in the
movement, which bears the name of Romanticism, which Rousseau
initiated. Without Rousseau there would have been no Shelley, no Keats,
no Goethe and no Byron.

Rousseau was not a poet – although he had a go at this genre as well
(Riley 2001: 3).[11] Unlike the preachers and the poets who gave sermons
against scientism, Rousseau, as a philosopher, gave 'reasons'. 'They have
perceived the evil, and I lay bare its causes and above all I point to something highly consoling and useful by showing that all these vices belong
not so much to man, as to man badly governed', he wrote in *Preface to
Narcissus* (II: 969). Though a cultural critic, Rousseau saw himself as a
political scientist – a man who had identified the source of evil in political
causes.

It is not difficult to find evidence of the same despair over the inexora-
ble progression of what Keats called the 'dull catalogue of common things'.
In *Letter to Voltaire* (written in response to the latter's charge that God
could not be almighty and good if he permitted the earthquake in Lisbon
1755), Rousseau made a point of noting that the disaster did 'not make
[him] doubt for a moment the immortality of the soul and a beneficent
providence' (Gourevitch 2001: 219). Rousseau was a religious man, indeed a Christian in an age of scientific reasoning, although his theological
views were hardly complex or sophisticated: '... I serve God with the simplicity of my heart' (Rousseau 1979a: 308). As a commentator has put it,
for Rousseau, the 'essence of Christianity lies in the preaching of a truth
that is immediate' (Starobinski 1988: 69). Or, as he himself put it, in his
Observations:

> The Divine book [*ce divin Livre*] is the only book the Christians need, and
> the most useful of all books even for those who might not be Christians,
> only needs to be mediated to convey to the soul the love of its author, and
> the will to carry its precepts. Never did virtue speak in such terms; never

did the deepest wisdom express itself with such energy and simplicity. One never leaves off reading it without feeling a better person than before. (III: 48–9)

This was not a popular view among the philosophers, at a time when Laplace had stated that he did not need the hypothesis of God in his system. Rousseau's personal profession of faith could be summed up in the maxim that God is good and the soul is immortal. Not exactly a majority opinion at a time when most philosophers took Voltaire's side in the debate over Lisbon,[12] and at a time when the bulk of the intellectuals sided with Hume's agnostic view that 'by the light of reason it seems difficult to prove the immortality of the soul' (Hume 1985: 591), Rousseau went against the common trend. While having declared that he would give reasons for his views, Rousseau did not care much for proofs, nor did he succumb to doubt and despair: 'doubt is too violent a feeling. As my reason is shaken, my creed cannot bear the tension and decides against reason' (IV: 1070). Such statements of Christian – albeit non-conformist[13] – beliefs did not however imply that his views were well received by the church. Christian thinkers – in his own day as well as after – have found it difficult to take Rousseau to their hearts,[14] perhaps because he (again like Kierkegaard) expressed himself through 'indirect communication', i.e. through the medium of fictional characters. Just as one is never sure if it is Shakespeare or Hamlet who speaks to us, we are never quite sure if Rousseau speaks to us, or if the voices of Wolmer, Julie or the Savoyard Vicar do. Unfortunately for Rousseau – and perhaps not entirely without justification – critics have identified Rousseau's religious views with that of the Savoyard Vicar.[15] Whatever his subsequent explanations Rousseau never denied that he – at least in large measure – shared the view of the fictional cleric. And this character did not, to put it mildly, soothe the views of official Christendom. While arguing (strongly) that 'the world is governed by a powerful and wise will' (Rousseau 1979a: 276) and confessing that 'the holiness of the Gospel speaks to the heart' (307), he seemed to suggest almost Humean agnosticism when letting the Vicar declare that 'the Gospel is full of unbelievable things, of things repugnant to reason and impossible for any sensible man to conceive or accept' (308). It is not surprising – nor unjustified – that this sentence brought down the wrath of the clerical establishment in Rome as well as in Geneva. Having elsewhere (for example in *Lettre à Voltaire*) taken the line of William Ockham, i.e. *credo ut absurdum*, Rousseau now seemed to have succumbed to *non credo ut non-intelligam*. Or did he? He subsequently, in *Lettre à Chistophe Beaumont*, argued that he had not defended the rationalist position, indeed, he had 'sought to combat modern materialism [and] to establish the existence of God' (cited in Cranston 1997: 50). And there is textual evidence to support this argument. In fact, the thrust of his argument in the *Profession of Faith of the Savoyard Vicar* is perhaps better summed up in the call for his readers to follow their inner voice: 'respect in silence what one can neither reject or understand, and humble yourself before the Great Being' (Rousseau 1979a: 308). That is, to submit oneself to God even when the Supreme Being's existence might contradict reason. This is not the profession of an agnostic but that of an individual who is willing to take the leap of faith.[16]

Rejecting the teachings of his erstwhile friends – whose views he never shared on this subject – Rousseau set out to fight a lonely battle against modernity and for Christianity, albeit his own personal understanding of this creed.

Life and work

Friedrich Nietzsche (Froese 2001) – who could control his enthusiasm for Rousseau – entitled one of the chapters in *Ecce Homo* 'Why I write such Great Books'. Not, it should be added, because of his personal merits – the reverse if anything – but because his personal failings were compensated for by the greatness of his work; '*das Eine bin ich, das Andere sind meine Schriften*' ('I am one thing, my writings something very different') (Nietzsche 1969: 296). The same, it seems, is true for Rousseau; a great writer – not an admirable individual. Casanova (not that he was in a position to preach!) noted that Rousseau 'was not what I could call a pleasant man' (Casanova 1968: 223).

We know it all; how he sent his children to the foundling home;[17] how he stole a ribbon – and blamed the misdeed on a poor girl (who suffered a cruel punishment) (I: 86); and how he abandoned a man who suffered a fit (I: 130). This is not a flattering self-portrait. Yet, it is important to remember that the main source of information is his own writings. His letters (he wrote about ten thousand) tell a rather different story.[18] These letters tell a story of a man anxious to secure a pension for his simple – and it seems beloved – companion Thérèse Levasseur, and of a man with a genuine concern for the weak and unfortunate members of society. Could it be that Rousseau exaggerated? Could it be that his self-professed indiscretions, which so appealed his critics, were less than accurate?

Rousseau had won instant fame for his prize essay in 1750 (I: 356). Two years later he presented his first opera to Louis XV (I: 384). He was subsequently offered a life pension. He rejected it! It must have been quite a turnaround for an impoverished foreigner (who had suffered indignity and humiliation throughout the 1740s) that he, within a few months, was catapulted to fame and the prospect of fortune. Celebrated, revered and feted, he now corresponded with princes, kings and the major thinkers of the day (Gourevitch 1997a).

It would be inaccurate in the extreme to suggest that Rousseau sought to please – or indeed flatter – his audience. He was not a sycophant. He noted in *Confessions* that he wore an unbrushed wig and had failed to shave when he presented his *Le Devin du Village* for the king. It seems that this added to the interest of his work! Nor did he make any efforts to please his colleagues among the composers and musicians in France.

French intellectual life has canonised Rousseau, laid his remains at Partheon, and re-named the street where he lived from *Rue Platrière* to *Rue de Jean-Jacques Rousseau* (Holmsten 1972: 48). It is hard to believe that the French – a people anxiously protecting and propagating the beauty of their language – have thus celebrated a man who attacked the ugliness of this very language in *Lettre sur la musique française*.[19]

It was as if Rousseau's accession to the status of philosophical celebrity prompted him to offend everybody. As if his repeated sufferings and humiliations somehow had to be repaid, as if he somehow had to settle the score with lesser minds. Yet it is also noteworthy that he never resorted to personal attacks or backstabbing. Rousseau is an enigma, perhaps because we know so much about him. He sought fame, yet he publicly decried it. He rejected vanity – or *amour propre* as he called it. Yet he also wanted to succeed in the Parisian *salons* – and he certainly enjoyed himself there (Cranston 1991: 5). He sang the praises of the rural life, but did not settle in Geneva.

The city of Geneva reinstated his citizenship in 1755 – after the publication of his *Discourse on Inequality* (which contained a preface which praised the city). Rousseau, however, did not seem anxious to practice what he what he had preached in his *Discourse*. Further, he later noted that he was upset that the city of his birth had admitted Voltaire to live in Geneva. 'I knew', wrote Rousseau, 'that this man would cause a revolution that I should find again in my own country the tore, the airs, and the manners which drove me from Paris' (I: 396). This, at any rate, is what he wrote in the *Confessions*. The view was different at the time, or so it seems. His hostility towards Voltaire was less pronounced, non-existent even, in the mid-1750s. Rousseau had, in fact, written a rather cordial letter to Voltaire – and this happened after the latter had written his scornful (or was it merely witty?) remark about the *Discourse on Inequality*:

Never has so much intelligence been deployed in an effort to make us beasts. One wants to walk on all fours after reading your book, but since I lost that habit more than sixty years ago, I fear I cannot recover it. (Voltaire 1973: 179)

In fact, it seems that many of Rousseau's antipathies were of a later date. Rather than reacting with characteristic fury to Voltaire's intention of moving to Geneva, Rousseau wrote a respectful letter which deserves to be quoted:

Monsieur, I must thank you in every way ... being sensible of the honour you have done to my country, I share the gratitude of my fellow citizens, which I hope will be all the greater when they have profited from the instruction which you are able to give them. (*Correspondance Complète* Vol. III: 319)

Rousseau even remarked that it had been his 'duty' as a writer to 'render homage' to a man whom he called 'our leader' (III: 319).

The story somehow doesn't add up. Was Rousseau talking about the same man? Was this the individual who would 'cause a revolution' in Geneva? Or, more incriminating, was the professed 'man of truth' trying to flatter his philosophical foe by dressing up as something that he was not (a believer in progress)? Perhaps not. In the letter Rousseau went on to say that progress had increased man's corruption (319), yet he remained cordial and respectful. The contemptuous feud between the two great men was of a later date.

So why did Rousseau go back to France? We might get part of the answer in a letter he wrote to Jean Jallabert – a noted scholar, physician and supporter of Rousseau against his (many) critics in Geneva. The reason is simple; Rousseau could not get a job in Geneva. The rustic paradise did not provide job opportunities for a note-copier; 'I have absolutely not a Sou to live on' (*Correspondance Complète* III: 336). Further, Rousseau was not unaware of the limitations on the public intellectual in the conservative Calvinist stronghold. The clerics did not have a history of toleration – as Rousseau was to find out when *Emile* was burned publicly following its publication in 1762. France, while still an autocracy, had an altogether more lax attitude to censorship.

Upon his return from Geneva he moved to L'Ermitage – a resort owned by Louise-Florence d'Epinay (a wealthy Parisian woman with literary aspirations). It was here, in rural solitude, that he started to write his most formidable contributions to philosophy: *Emile*, *Du Contrat Social* and *La Nouvelle Héloïse*. But it was also at L'Ermitage that he became infatuated with Sophie d'Houdetot, Mme d'Epinay's sister-in-law. Rousseau – if we are to believe Hume (Hume 1932: 527) – was a ladies' man. In a memoir he wrote that 'all the great ladies teaze me to be introduced to him: I had *Rouleaus* thrust into my hand with earnest applications, that would prevail on him to accept them. I am persuaded, that were I to open here a subscription with his consent I should receive 50,000 pounds in a fortnight.' Perhaps surprisingly for an un-saintly figure like Rousseau, he did not take advantage of his charm. Indeed, his female companions (with the notable exception of Mme de Warrens) were notably simple (Thérèse Levasseur) or (reportedly) downright ugly. Sophie d'Houdetot – who infatuated him more than any other woman – was, he writes (in *Les Confessions* (I: 442), 'by no means handsome. Her face was pitted with smallpox, her complexion coarse, she was short sighted and her eyes were rather too round.' Yet her character was 'angelic, gentleness of the soul was the foundation of it'. It was to this woman that he wrote *Lettres Morales*, written out of an uncontrollable – and immoral – obsession which blinded his already deficient judgement and led to a break with his benefactress.

Rousseau was not an easy man to deal with. Nor was his friendship with the *philosophes* strong enough to endure his continued attacks on the central theses in their belief system. Rousseau – like Kierkegaard – was easy to offend. The latter suffered a nervous breakdown when Aron Goldschmidt's *Corsaren* depicted him as a hunchback.[20] Rousseau broke down when Diderot, in the play *Fils Naturel*, noted that 'I appeal to your heart, consult it, and it will tell you that the good man is part of society, only he is evil who lives alone' (Diderot 1994–97 IV: 1113). It did not help that Diderot, in a subsequent letter to his erstwhile friend, wrote, 'it is a rather odd citizen who is a hermit' (Diderot V: 63). Diderot had hit a raw nerve – but also one that prompted Rousseau to make his most lasting contributions.

Two disciplines in particular have benefited from the contributions of Rousseau; political science and education (Putterman 1999). In both cases the inspiration was conceived not in Montmorency (where he settled following his eviction from L'Ermitage), but in the 1740s when he had practical experiences with these matters.

We often fail to appreciate that Rousseau, like many others (Descartes, Hobbes, Spinoza, Marx and Locke come to mind), was a practical man, not an ivory tower theorist. Most contemporary thinkers are detached from the practical world; their concerns are theoretical in origin and abstract in outcome. The classics were not theoreticians by profession but by inclination. Machiavelli did not see himself as a philosopher but as a political practitioner; the same was true for Alexis de Tocqueville (a deputy and a foreign minister), John Stuart Mill (an MP), Karl Marx (a political activist), Edmund Burke (an MP) and the later American president James Madison. Rousseau belongs to this school of writers. Like many of his peers, he was not a paid up member of the intellectual elite, he was rather driven to write; to see the deeper significance in seemingly mundane things. It is perhaps this more than anything else which is the hallmark of the genius. To earn a living Rousseau had worked as a tutor (and male nanny) for Mably's children – an ordeal, if we are to believe him, but one which inspired him to write *Emile*.

It is commonly assumed that Rousseau was a dreamer, a vagabond, *un reveur solitaire*. He was those as well, yet he was also an able practitioner (his diplomatic dispatches, printed in Vol. III of *Oeuvres Complètes*, are testament to this). And it is telling that it was his experiences as secretary at the French Embassy in Venice which inspired him to write *Du Contrat Social* – not abstract considerations or armchair theorising. Of course he was not alone in this. The English Civil War prompted Hobbes to take up his pen, just as social inequality prompted Marx to follow suit. The list could go on indefinitely.

Rousseau was a successful writer, at least when measured by his influence. Yet his masterpieces were not well received by his contemporaries, and still less by his compatriots. Rousseau was expelled from France following the publication of *Emile*, and in Geneva the book was burned by the public prosecutor. His misfortunes began in June 1762. At two o'clock in the morning on the ninth of that month, Rousseau received a note from the Duchess of Luxembourg. The message was as simple as it was alarming; the *Grand Chambre* would – the following day – issue a warrant for his arrest. He immediately decided to flee. He summoned Thérèse to tell her the bad news. He later recalled telling his companion, 'you have shared the good days of my prosperity. It now remains for you, since you wish it, to share my miseries. Expect nothing but insults and disasters henceforth. The fate that begins for me on this unhappy day will pursue me to the last hour of my life' (I: 583). This prediction was sadly accurate.

His sin – which he rejected and refuted in *Lettres écrites de la montagne* – was the alleged godlessness of his fictional character the 'Savoyard Vicar'. Did he expect this? Was he prepared for these – in part self-inflicted – sufferings? Almost certainly not. So why did he suffer this plight? One can distinguish between three aspects of a philosopher's work: what the author wanted to write; what he actually wrote; and how the writings are read.[21] Rousseau was misunderstood, possibly because what he wrote was different from what he intended to write, but possibly also because it was convenient for the authorities to have a scapegoat on whom to blame all evil.[22] As a public intellectual Rousseau was a useful tool for politicians – and this was exploited in the internal politics, not least in Geneva, where the elite used the publication of *Emile* as a pretext for tightening of the laws on censorship.

It was almost certainly this adversity which led Rousseau into what resembles madness. Yet his madness – if it may be called such – was never the only mood (and it is, therefore, questionable if his condition meets the requirement of a mental disorder as defined by psychiatrists). Pathological depressions are characterised by a continued and relentless state of mental paralysis. Rousseau's condition was not like that. Having escaped to Neuchatel, and subsequently to Isle de Saint Pierre, he found time to write *Projet sur la constitution de la Corse*, a thoughtful application of his political philosophy requested by the insurgent Corsican government.

It is possible that Rousseau exacerbated the hostility towards him. Yet one cannot in fairness accuse a man of paranoia who has suffered the indignity of being dispelled from three countries, and whose house has been stoned by the angry mob – as was the case in Môtiers (Cranston 1997: 116). But maybe Rousseau suffered more because he reacted more strongly than other philosophers. His fate was not unlike that of other great minds similarly condemned to be fugitives. That is writers who, like Plato, Thomas Aquinas, Sigmund Freud, Thomas Hobbes, Nicolo Machiavelli, John Locke, Albert Einstein and Karl Marx, had to seek refuge for fear of the consequences of their writings. What is certain is that Rousseau – being a novelist as much as a philosopher – was perversely inspired by his sufferings, and transformed these sufferings to his autobiographical writings. Adversity certainly did his philosophical writings no favours. His major philosophical works were conceived and produced in tranquillity. His autobiographical works, on the other hand, were the result of mental suffering and political repression.

No wonder Rousseau fascinated, and as the continued output of books on his life suggest, continues to fascinate. His life, as much as his books, appeals to us because he could transform despair into prose; sufferings into eloquence.

We are seeking guidance at a time where there is none, and so we reach back to the age of the giants – the titans of our species who may teach us. In old Norse mythology there is a word for these figures – a *Skjald*. That is someone who, like Dostoevsky, Francis of Assisi, Virgil, Dante or Shakespeare, has travelled to the twilight-zone beyond good and evil, and who has returned to reveal their insights in myths and tales. Rousseau is the *Skjald*, the writer who has diagnosed the malady of the modern age, and transformed it into prose. We do not seek to measure men, still less to rank them against each other. We merely strive to learn from their trials and tribulations – and in this we can seek solace in the works of Rousseau. On 2 June 1778, Rousseau died in Ermenonville. He was laid to rest on the Isle de Peupliers. Rousseau lived and died, but death did not end it. It was Rousseau's fate in life as well as in death to be an instrument of political expediency. In the early 1770s, the French government sought to utilise Rousseau to kill two diplomatic birds with one philosopher's stone. Anxious to maintain the balance of power in Europe, the French government was alarmed by Russia's and Prussia's influence over Poland. Yet France was politically and militarily too weak to intervene. The government wanted to support the Council of the Bar (the noblemen opposed to the election of Stanislaw II as king of Poland), yet they feared the consequences of official association with the insurgents. They shared their aspirations, yet were rightly doubtful of their chances of success. What could they do? Rousseau came in handy. The government offered Rousseau political asylum, on the condition that he refrained from writing about politics, and then asked him to do exactly this; to write a proposal for a constitutional settlement in Poland (in secrecy, that is).

The Poles had expected more but could hardly reject the offer of expert advise from the most famous philosopher of the time. Louis XV, on his part, could dissociate himself from involvement by pointing to Rousseau's madness, and at the same time support his allies. And so it came to pass that Rousseau, out of political expediency, wrote his last work of political philosophy, *Considérations sur le gouvernement de Pologne et sur sa réformation projettée* (1771).

The republican Rousseau's reputation came in handy for the monarchical regime. The same was true for the populist tyrants after the French revolution. Deceased political thinkers have one pre-eminent recommendation; they do not object to the abuse of their ideas. 'It is Rousseau's fault', said one of the characters in *Les Misérables*. And the fictional character can be excused for reaching this conclusion. Yet it is perhaps more accurate to say that it was Robespierre's fault. More than anyone Maximilien de Robespierre, architect of the terror regime of the French Revolution, is responsible for having created the noxious Rousseau. At the height of his powers, in 1792, the demagogue presented himself as the self-anointed incarnation of the General Will. Addressing the Jacobins he confidently declared; 'For us, we are not of any faction … our will is the General Will' (cited in O'Brien 2002: 301). It is difficult to exaggerate the amount of damage done to Rousseau's name by this statement.

Robespierre's death did not alter Rousseau's position; the new regime needed him just as much as the previous one had. Declaring that Robespierre had 'falsified Rousseau and that they themselves were the true heirs' (O'Brien 2002: 302), they even strengthened the cult. The revolutionaries wasted no time in squeezing political capital out of Rousseau's corpse. Anxious to acquire legitimacy for their regime, they exhumed the remains of the celebrated ideologue and brought his body to Paris where, by cruel irony, his coffin was placed next to Voltaire's. On the way to the Partheon – the converted church of Sainte Genevieve – a large crowd had assembled. It is reported that they chanted '*Vive la mémoire de Jean-Jacques Rousseau!*'

Notes

1 The biographical literature on Rousseau is vast. The following works are frequently cited: Raymond Trousson, *Jean-Jacques Rousseau: heurs et malheurs d'une conscience* (Paris: Hachette, 1993); Raymond Trousson, *Jean-Jacques Rousseau* (Paris: Tallandier, 1988–89), 2 vols; Jean Guéhenno, *Jean-Jacques Rousseau* (Paris: Grasset, puis Gallimard, 1948–1952), 3 vols; Bernard Gagnebin (ed.), *La rencontre de Jean-Jacques Rousseau* (Genève: Georg, 1962); Marc-Vincent Howlett, *Jean-Jacques Rousseau: l'homme qui croyait en l'homme* (Paris: Gallimard 'Découvertes', 1989); Michel Soëtard, *Jean-Jacques Rousseau* (Genève et Lucerne: Coeckelberghs, 1989); Gavin De Beer, *Jean-Jacques Rousseau and his World* (New York: Putnam's Sons, 1972); Maurice Cranston, *Jean-Jacques: The Early Life and Work of Jean-Jacques Rousseau, 1712–1754* (New York: Norton, 1983); Maurice Cranston, *The Noble Savage: Jean-Jacques Rousseau, 1754–1762* (Chicago: University of Chicago Press, 1991); Lester G. Crocker, *Jean-Jacques Rousseau* (New York: Macmillan, 1968–73), 2 vols.

2 A fact which, if anything, is indicated by weighty extensions to the already impressive literature about Rousseau: Patrick Riley, *The Cambridge Companion to Rousseau* (Cambridge: Cambridge University Press, 2002); Maurice Cranston, *The Solitary Self: Jean-Jacques Rousseau in Exile and Adversity* (Chicago: University of Chicago Press, 1997); Christopher Kelly, *Rousseau's Exemplary Life: The Confessions as Political Philosophy* (London: Cornell University Press, 1987); Robert Wokler's brief but succinct *Rousseau: A Very Short Introduction* (Oxford: Oxford University Press, 2001), R.A. Leigh's collection of *all* Rousseau's letters in *Correspondance Complète de Jean-Jacques Rousseau* (Geneva and Oxford: Voltaire Foundation, 1965–), 53 vols, which finally allows us to pass judgement on his autobiographical writings, and the now complete Pléiade edition of his *Oeuvres Complètes* (Gallimard: Bibliothèque de la Pléiade, 1959–95), 5 vols. This will be cited by volume number followed by page number, e.g. III: 96, means Volume 3, page 96).

3   See, for example, 'Rousseau et la Révolution' in *Études Jean-Jacques Rousseau* (Reims: Editions 'l'Écart', 1987–), Musée Jean-Jacques Rousseau de Montmorency.

4   Aldous Huxley commented on this subject: 'if you have behaved badly, repent, make what amends you can and address yourself to the task of behaving better next time. On no account brood over your wrongdoing. Rolling in the muck is not the best way of getting clean.' Huxley, 'Foreword', in *Brave New World* (London: HarperCollins, 1994 [1932]), p. 1.

5   See Rousseau's letter to his father in 1731 in Leigh (ed.), *Correspondance Complète*, Vol. I, p. 11.

6   The first mention of his abandonment of his children is in a letter to Mme de Francueil in 1751. His own account of the story in *Les Confessions* can be found at Vol. I, pp. 1416–22.

7   Though interested readers may wish to consult Philip Robinson, *Jean-Jacques Rousseau's Doctrine of the Arts* (Berne, 1984) and R. Wokler, *Rousseau on Society, Politics, Music and language. An Historical Interpretation of his Early Writings* (New York: Garland, 1987).

8   Diderot's support for his friend has greatly puzzled scholars. Gita May offers this reflection; 'One can but wonder why Diderot did not immediately recognise the *Discourse on the Sciences and the Arts* as a clear and flagrant repudiation of everything the *Encyclopédie* stood for. Indeed he did everything in his power to promote the success of the *Discourse*. Perhaps it was because he was a loyal, generous, and steadfast friend eager to see Rousseau's essay win the price, but perhaps also because he not only admired Rousseau's rhetorical virtuosity but also subconsciously acknowledged that the darker more ominous message of the *Discourse* deserved to be taken seriously'. Gita May, 'Rousseau, Cultural Critic', in Susan Dunn (ed.), *The Social Contract and the First and Second Discourses* (New Haven: Yale University Press, 2002), p. 263.

9   There are several similarities between Kierkegaard and Rousseau, although few studies compare the two. The classic study remains Ronald Grimsley's 'Kierkegaard and Rousseau', in Grimsley, *Søren Kierkegaard and French Literature* (Oxford: Oxford University Press, 1966).

10 It should be noted that Voltaire parted company with the other philosophers of the Enlightenment on the subject of religion. Voltaire developed a philosophy that saw Newton's physics as a manifestation of the glory of God. 'The whole philosophy of Newton leads necessarily to the knowledge of a Supreme Being, who created everything, arranged everything of his own free will'. Voltaire quoted in N. Hampson, *The Enlightenment* (London: Penguin, 1990), p. 79. Yet – as is well-known – he did not believe that God was all-powerful or good. Scepticism regarding the latter was the theme of *Candide*.

11 An example of his poetry is *Le Verger des Charmettes*: '*Tantot avec Leibniz, Malabrance et Newton/Je monte ma raison sur un sublime ton/j'examine les lois des corps et des pénses/avec Locke je fais l'histoire des idées*', quoted in P.

Riley, 'Introduction: The Life and Works of Jean-Jacques Rousseau (1712–1778)', in Riley (ed.), *The Cambridge Companion to Rousseau* (Cambridge: Cambridge University Press, 2001b).

12 However, Immanuel Kant was the exception: the Prussian wrote, 'After Newton and Rousseau, God is justified, and Pope's thesis is henceforth true' (Kant quoted in V. Gourevitch. 'The Religious Thought', in Riley (ed.), *The Cambridge Companion to Rousseau*, p. 193).

13 See Harald Høffding, *Rousseau und Seine Philosophie* (Stuttgart: Fr. Frommanns Verlag, 1910), p. 127.

14 The Archbishop of Paris, Beaumont, complained that Rousseau's language was 'at complete variance with the doctrine of Holy Scripture and of the Church concerning the revolution which has come about in our nature', Christophe de Beaumont, *Mandement, portant condamnation d'un livre qui a pour titre EMILE OU DE L'EDUCATION …*', quoted in O'Hagan, 1999, *Rousseau*, London, Routledge, pp. 241–2.

15 The vicar is, of course a literary character. Yet, as Roger Masters has noted, 'Rousseau … explicitly acknowledges the view of the vicar as similar, though not identical to his own' (*The Political Philosophy of Rousseau* (Princeton: Princeton University Press, 1968), p. 55). N.J.H. Dent believes that 'there is no doubt that the vicar's views are his own'. N.J.H. Dent, *Rousseau Dictionary* (Blackwell: Oxford, 1992), p. 77. Rousseau himself wrote that the result of his research on 'religious matters was more or less [*à peu près*] what I have written down in my Profession of Faith of the Savoyard Vicar' (III: 55). Yet at other times he seemed to distance himself from the views of the vicar, for example in *Letters écrites de la Montagne*, where he denounces the views of the vicar as 'fictional' (III: 750).

16 Again Kierkegaard comes to mind. In *Concluding Unscientific Postscript* (Afsluttende Uvidenskabelig Efterskrift), the Dane wrote: 'the existence of God follows from the leap'. Søren Kierkegaard, *Afsluttende Uvidenskabelig Efterskrift*, in Kierkegaard, *Samlede Værker* (Copenhagen: Gyldendal, 1991), vol. 9, p. 15.

17 This singular fact was revealed by Voltaire. There is no reason to doubt that it was true. It is interesting that Rousseau, in his *Fragments Politiques*, cites a statistic showing that 5,082 of the 19,202 children born in Paris in 1758 had been handed over to the foundling home (III: 528).

18 Fortunately these are now all available thanks to the late R.A. Leigh's lifetime achievement, the collection of the *Correspondance Complète de Jean-Jacques Rousseau*.

19 His attack was part of a musical dispute, which has later become known as the *Querelle des Bouffons*. The dispute had erupted in August 1752; Rousseau entered the debate in 1753. He argued that Italian music, based on melody and voice, was closer to the moral, meaningful, nature of music. French music, by contrast, was not. The differentiated sound worlds of the French language and French music, argued Rousseau, revealed a process of disintegration.

20 On Rousseau and Kierkegaard see Harvie Fergusson, *Melancholy and the Critique of Modernity* (Routledge: London, 1995), p. 63.

21 I owe this observation to professor Rodney Barker, LSE.

22 Réné Girard has developed a theory of the sociological 'need' for scapegoats. 'In Greek mythology, the scapegoat is never wrongfully accused. But he is always magical. He has the capacity to relieve the burden of guilt from society. This seems a basic human impulse. There is a need to consume scapegoats. It is the way tension is relieved and change takes place.' This might – or might not – fit Rousseau's case. (Girard quoted in J. Klein, *The Natural. The Misunderstood Presidency of Bill Clinton* (New York: Coronet, 2002), p. 184).

2

The disenchantment of the world

> War on his temples, do not all charms fly
> At the mere touch of cold philosophy
> There once was a rainbow in heaven
> We know her woof, her texture, she is given
> In the dull catalogue of common things
> Philosophy will clip an angel's wings
> Conquer all the mysteries by rule and line
> Empty the haunted air, and gnomed mine
> Unweave the rainbow, as it erstwhile made
> The tender person'd Lamia melt into a shade
> (John Keats, *Lamia*, Part II, ll. 229–37)

Keats wrote these lines in the early part of the nineteenth century. Yet, it is questionable if the Englishman would have expressed himself in this way had it not been for Jean-Jacques Rousseau.[1] More than any other writer, Rousseau became the apostle of the romantic reaction against vain scientism and the intellectual hubris of the Enlightenment. Strangely, perhaps, as Rousseau in the same period was treated as the intellectual father of the French Revolution, and as he – according to Joseph De Maistre and Edmund Burke – was to blame for the demise of the traditional order. To be sure, great men invite different interpretations. Yet, it is difficult in fairness to accuse Rousseau of having sought to undermine the metaphysical foundations of the established order. (We shall argue below that Burke and Rousseau, in fact, shared the same view on the 'disenchantment of the world'.) Rousseau – the 'noble savage' among the 'philosophers' – was nothing if not a critic of progress and enlightenment.

And it is for this reason that he may be judged irrelevant today. More than ever the doctrine of progress stands unopposed. Haven't we achieved the final phase of history? Is there any society better than the secular welfare state? Where would we be without the progress of medical technologies and the tremendous advances in the sciences, which have led to electricity, the lap-top computer, MTV, the electric guitar, Viagra, Boeing 747s, the hedonistic pleasures of the welfare state and cellular phones? Have we ever had it so good? Brave new world! What more could we possibly want?

The history of progress

Certainly the sciences have made life easier in many respects. Yet it is as if there is a flaw in the heaven of progress, as if something is not quite as it was meant to be. We are no longer frightened by serpents, the eternal pyres of Hell, we no longer burn witches – and thank God for that! Yet, the epoch that has been described as 'three centuries united by progress', has also had a downside. And in some ways, this down side has, perhaps, been as dark as the evils which science and knowledge were supposed to overcome. The modern epoch has brought us soap-operas, Prozac and the electrical toothbrush, but it has also brought us the nuclear bomb, CO_2 pollution, child pornography on the Internet, and totalitarian ideologies based on 'scientific' reasoning. This is the dark side to a development, which no one intended; applications of technologies established for the benefit of mankind, which turned against him.

This is a replay of the development in Rousseau's time. Armed with the insights of the scientific revolution, philosophers like Diderot, d'Alembert, Voltaire and d'Holbach set out to free mankind from its age-old cocoon of superstition and establish a more reasonable world of experiment and progress. While the great majority of the populations in Europe continued to accept the literal truth of the Bible and the existence of a Christian order, those in the forefront of the new scientific and intellectual movements had been 'alienated from a Church that insisted on the literal truth of revelation' (Hampson 1990: 94). It was left to d'Holbach, in his *Système de la nature*, to assert, with characteristic bluntness, that there was no divine purpose and no master plan:

> The whole cannot have an object, for outside itself there is nothing towards which it can tend … Men have completely failed to see that this nature, lacking both good and evil intentions, merely acts in accordance with necessary and immutable laws when it creates and destroys living things, from time to time making those suffer whom it created sentient, as it distributed good and evil among them. (d'Holbach quoted in Hampson 1990: 94)

Yet by 1800 this optimism about man and society had begun to evaporate – thanks mainly to the work of Rousseau (and later Goethe). In Rousseau's works there was discernible a new inner voice, and an awareness of the individual's uniqueness, which had eluded his colleagues.

It is still not customary to criticise progress. Conservatism is not a positive adjective in the early stages of the twenty-first century – nor was it in the middle of the eighteenth. Voltaire scornfully rebuked Rousseau's opposition to science and progress in *Discourse sur l'inégalité*, branding it Rousseau's 'second book against the human race' (Gray 1998: 38).[2] Yet, even in popular culture there have occasionally been criticisms of the unintended consequences of the evolution of technologies that take over the control of humans; Mary Shelley's *Frankenstein* is not that different from Arnold Schwarzenegger's *Terminator*. Works of varying intellectual merit, to be sure, but both expressions of the same concern; that technologies have taken control – to the detriment, rather than to the benefit, of mankind. (A fact which, more than anything, is evident in the history of warfare. As military historian John Keegan (1993: 359–61) has shown, the increasing number of casualties in wars – civilian as well as non-civilian – is a direct consequence of technological developments.) They never intended it to happen in this way. The scientists who reacted against clerical reaction and supposition were not what Rousseau was later to term 'evangelists of atheism' (Stiebing 1993: 32). Rather they were God-fearing men of considerable theological sophistication. Isaac Newton wrote more about theology than about mathematics; Mendel, the father of modern genetics, was a pious monk; Blaise Pascal was a religious thinker more than a mathematician and a physicist; Johannes Kepler was a mystic as well as an astronomer, as was Copernicus. Nicolas Steno – the father of modern palaeontology and geology – was an ordained priest, so too was Bruno. Being a heretic was not a pre-qualification for entering into the premier league of great scientific minds – but a degree in divinity seemed a good starting point (indeed, even Charles Darwin acquired one!). But the new creed was a threat to the established order – an order which, paradoxically, had been weakened by the Reformation initiated by pious souls like Martin Luther and Jean Calvin. While the God-fearing intentions of these two men were beyond dispute, the consequence of their revolt was a wholly unintended secularisation. Summing up this development Max Weber concluded that 'the fate of our times is characterised by rationalism and intellectualisation, and above all the disenchantment [*entzauberung*] of the world' (Weber 1997: 155).[3] Even Friedrich Nietzsche, in so many ways the evangelist of atheism, could empathise with the *Angst* and the gruesome prospect of *horror vacui*. In *The Joyful Science* Nietzsche wrote the story of the madman, a tale which leaves nobody in doubt about how disturbing the author found God's death:

> We have killed him [God] you and I! We are all his murderers. But how have we done it? How could we swallow the sea? Who gave us the sponge to rub the entire horizon? What were we when we unchained the Earth from the Sun? Where is it going? Where are we going? Away from all suns? Are we hurling straight downwards? And backwards, sideways, forwards, in all directions? Is there still an up and down? Are we drifting through infinite nothing? (Nietzsche 1994: 125)

The scientists and the religious reformists had sought to encourage a deeper love of God. Much to their horror, their findings were seized upon by their enemies as arguments against that very belief system which they supported. Agnostics, and outright atheists, skilfully used the writings of the early scientists to sow the seeds of doubt. Not, it should be said, for devious reasons (though religious fanatics are certain to suggest that), but for the benefit of mankind. Equipped with the tools and insight of science, modern progressives like Hobbes, Hume, Diderot, Helvetius and d'Alembert – to mention but a few – saw that God was no longer needed in order to create a better world. While Christ remained a revered character – and a model for emulation even for atheists – Christendom was no longer needed to secure the benefits of everyone. Rather the Church had prevented progress that (even then) had brought benefits for mankind – or those of them who could afford such modern wonders and benefit from the new understanding of the human body begun by the likes of Harvey and Paracelsus. They – ie. the scientists – had a point. The Church – Protestant as well as Catholic – got bad press from trying to suppress scientists like Galileo, Bruno and Spinoza. Furthermore, relief from the prospects of a miserable afterlife (as described in Dante's *Inferno*) must have seemed refreshing for even the staunchest believer.

It was against the backdrop of these developments that Rousseau took up his pen in 1749, to write his *Discourse sur les sciences et les arts*. The work was not, he would later admit, 'one of my best', yet, perhaps, was still his most forceful contribution to the history of the ideas, providing, as it did, the first assault on a creed that had already become the dominant one in the collective psyche of Western society.

We have already recounted the events that prompted him to enter into the Republic of Letters – albeit as a disloyal subject! It serves little purpose to repeat a story so well-known. What remains an open question, however, is whether Rousseau's opposition to the plight of modernity – and his advocacy of a simple (Christian) philosophy is a credible one – and not merely one that can be confined to the dustbin of dated doctrines of a bygone age. Rousseau was not the first thinker to advocate a traditional view (Pascal had done the same), neither was Rousseau the first to reject the prevailing positivist doctrine. Nor, for that matter, was he the last to do so (Kierkegaard was later to strike similar chords). But Rousseau was possibly the most eloquent – and the most misunderstood – of the anti-modernists.[4]

John Locke, not normally regarded as an anti-modernist, warned against the challenge of the atheist philosophers in *The Reasonableness of Christianity:* 'Collect all the moral rules of philosophers and compare them with those contained in the New Testament', he wrote, continuing, '[the doctrines of the philosophers would] fall short of the morality delivered by our Saviour and taught to his Apostles, a College made up for the most part of ignorant but inspired fishermen' (Locke 1965: 217–18). A pre-modern view, perhaps, but one which has also been expressed by a modern thinker like Alistair MacIntyre who, in *After Virtue*, noted that the Enlightenment project had 'failed by its own standards, since its pro-tagonists had never succeeded in specifying a uniquely justifiable set of principles to which any fully rational agent whatsoever could not fail to assent' (MacIntyre 1989: 271).[5] This view seems reasonable – if not undisputed – today. August Comte's confident belief in the 'unquestionable superiority of demonstrated [i.e. scientific] morals over revealed morals', is no longer in vogue (Comte 1854: 356).

Yet, while other (prominent) writers have raged similarly against the seemingly unquestioned and unchallenged advances of scientism, Rousseau remains the most forceful, and least compromising, of the challengers. Not merely because of his eloquence but also because of his tenacity of purpose and his ceaseless insistence that the Enlightenment, which was to free man, has trapped and imprisoned him in a disenchanted, Godless world. As he put it: 'To wrest all belief in God from mens' heart is to destroy all virtue in it' (IV: 1144). Religion – and for Rousseau this meant Christianity – was not merely an ethical doctrine but a metaphysical 'truth'. God *had* sent His son to redeem the world. Jesus was not merely a symbolic figure along the lines of Socrates; 'if the life and death of Socrates are those of a sage, the life and death of Jesus are those of a God' (IV: 625). This view was as strange to the *Philosophes* as it is to their present-day heirs. In more ways than one everything has changed and yet remained the same. The 'ardent missionaries of atheism' still confidently predict the demise of religion, the belief in the afterlife, the existence of God, and 'ordinary' men and women still worship – while scientific theories are being falsified. It was this hubris that Rousseau sought to combat – and it was this that brought down the wrath of the proto-positivist thinkers of his day. Yet, while Rousseau was a 'gospel Christian' (at least by his own definition), he was also preoccupied with the moral and political implications of secularism. Especially the development (or demise) of ethical theory after Hobbes. It is not least because of this that he is of interest to the modern science of politics. Rousseau rejected the Hobbesian view. In opposition to his colleagues he maintained that the 'summation of all morality is given by the Gospel in its summation of the Law' (III: 155–6).

The poverty of neo-liberalism

Nobody in the political mainstream speaks out against capitalism today. Opposition to free markets is seen as naive – or a proof of ignorance of the laws of economics. Hibernating or moribund Marxists of a Gramscian hue may talk about a 'hegemonic project', others – however reluctantly – may admit to Fukuyama's thesis of the 'End of History' (Fukuyama 1992); that world history, ideologically speaking, has ended, that liberalism has triumphed. Scores of reports trumpet the virtues of the prevailing system of market capitalism – and are followed up by prophecies proving that Adam Smith's 'invisible hand' will ensure a *Pareto*-optimal allocation of resources to the benefit of all. As always the empirical evidence in support of the utopian prospects is thin – if not, as in this case, almost wholly absent.[6] Indeed, the *Financial Times*, hardly a basher of capitalism, concluded that twenty years of capitalism had resulted in growing inequalities: 'in 1980 the top 1 per cent of American households owned a quarter of the American wealth: by the late 1990s, that single percentage owned more than 38 per cent' (*Financial Times*, 17 August 2002). Figures from the global economy showed an even greater – and growing – divide between rich and poor. And, just as the rich were getting richer, the poor were getting (much) poorer. Even the World Bank has conceded that 'it is the rich who benefit from globalisation' (World Bank 2002: 1). In 1990 2.7 billion people were living on less than US$2 a day. Ten years later this number had grown by one hundred million people.[7] The poor get poorer.

The legacy of vulgar capitalism was one of a belief in the automatic society. But its proponents were also ideologues with a particular philosophical outlook. Free marketers – not unlike 'scientific socialists' –

argue that we must endure the hardship (of IMF conditionals) before we can rest in the free marketer nirvana of the *minimal state*. It has taken a long while for this system to be established. It is testament to Marx' predictive powers that what he foresaw in the 1840s has finally materialised in the early decades of the twenty-first century. The new creed of WTO-induced global capitalism has – and here we invoke Marx:

> torn asunder the motley feudal ties that bound man to his natural superiors, and has left remaining no other nexus between man and man than naked self-interest, than callous cash payment. It has drowned the most heavenly ecstasies of religious fervour … in the icy water of egotistical calculation. It has resolved personal worth into exchange value, and in place of the numberless indefeasible chartered freedoms, has set up that single unconscionable freedom – Free Trade. (Marx 1848: 82)

Alas the Rheinländer's predictive powers were stronger than his prescribed cure for the illness. Marx's diagnosis was, it seems, correct – the treatment was not! For like the free-marketer liberals, Marx sought to resolve the failings of capitalism with a misplaced faith in rationalism and social engineering. Like Richardo, Smith and Malthus, Marx sought to discern 'the laws of motion of modern society' in order to create a better world on the basis of this knowledge (Marx 1962, 15). Strangely for a would-be working-class hero, Marx never developed a philosophical argument for his social outrage. He never explained why capitalism was morally corrupt. He merely focused on the positive arguments. Marx was evidently concerned about the plight of the poor (chapter 40 in the *Capital* being a case in point), yet he never sought to underpin his observations with a philosophical theory of why political action was necessary to relieve the weak from their unjust hardship in a 'heartless world'. Like the free-marketers and utilitarians, Marx believed ethical considerations to be of a second order. Leave capitalism to itself, thought Marx, and it will give way to a better society. The current neo-liberals, scarcely less confident in their ideology, reason in much the same way; leave capitalism alone, and it will reach the panglosian best of all possible worlds. In both cases a belief in the objective laws of political economy has provided the theoreticians with the answer. And, in both cases self-interest was the key to understanding society. The utilitarians championed individual self-interest. This was especially true for Helvétius (Helvétius 1963: 204), who went on to become the main inspiration for Jeremy Bentham – and, indeed, Marx.[8] Bentham left no one in doubt about his position. In *An Introduction to the Principles of Morals and Legislation*, he wrote that 'nature has placed mankind under the governance of two sovereign masters; pain and pleasure. It is for them alone to point out what we *ought* to do' (Bentham 2000: 87, italics added). The Marxists, on their part, rested their theoretical faith on antagonistic class interests locked in a zero-sum game destined to end in the final victory for the proletariat. Arguably just another name for the same thing.

It seems fair to conclude that neither doctrine has produced the expected result. The legacy of decades of experiments with first socialism, and latterly capitalism, should leave few observers in doubt that these doctrines have failed to resolve all the ills of society. Certainly some problems have been resolved, yet others have emerged. We have not squared the politico-philosophical circle – Francis Fukuyama's obituary over world history not withstanding. This development would not have surprised Rousseau.

Modernity created a *Titanic* out of scientific hubris. The circumstances of the present crisis might be unique. Yet, the underlying pattern is the same as that which Rousseau rejected in the 1750s. Like the *Soothsayer of the Village*, in his opera of that name, the Genevan foresaw that modernity, rather than liberating man, has locked him up in a system from which there is no escape, no prospect of a blissful afterlife, and no salvation. A world of hedonism and run-amok materialism. Rousseau's lamentations about the decline of spirituality (see the previous chapter), and his horror at the deification of selfishness, were what caused him to develop an alternative to the models which have prevailed since his own time.

The poverty of Hobbesianism

Nobody quite knows how it happened. No single philosopher, statesman or cleric can be blamed for the demise of the selfless ethics of the classics and of Christian religion. Yet one philosopher stands accused of putting the doctrine into writing; Thomas Hobbes (1588–1679). Hobbes – perhaps alongside Machiavelli – deserves (dis)credit for being the first major philosopher who sought to develop a moral philosophy on immoral foundations. The 'son of an otherwise undistinguished Wiltshire vicar' (Oakeshott 1991: 221) had somehow got it into his brilliant head that man was driven by egoism alone – and that all attempts at improving society would have to take this (regrettable) fact as its point of departure. In *Leviathan* he spelled out his chilling view of moral life, noting that 'whatsoever is the object of any mans Appetite or Desire; that is it, which he for his part calleth *Good*: And the object of his hate, and Aversion, *Evill*' (Hobbes 1650: 24). All human actions and attitudes towards other people were – in Hobbes' view – derived from these first principles. On the face of it an absurdly simplistic account, however not an unreasonable one for someone who had witnessed the atrocities of the Civil War. What is bizarre is that the Hobbes' philosophical heirs, above all Jeremy Bentham (2000: 87) – who had been spared the horrors of Cromwell's onslaught – followed the former in assuming that the human heart was driven by 'Appetite' and 'Desire'. Hobbes' model struck a chord; perhaps because of its extremely economical account, its stringent style, and his imitation of the cherished model of the natural sciences and Euclidean geometry. Rousseau had great respect for his adversary, yet he believed that:

> Hobbes' error was that … of having established that a state of war had existed between men who were independent and sociable, where he went wrong was in supposing that this state was natural to mankind and in considering it the cause of vices of which it is really the effect. (III: 288)

Selfishness – or *amour propre*, as he called it (see below) – was caused by a depraved society: it did not precede it. It would be natural to jump to the conclusion that Rousseau, therefore, regarded the state of nature as a blissful paradise of noble savages. And while he was – in weaker moments – inclined to express this view, it was not an opinion he expressed in his political and sociological writings. Morality did not exist in the state of nature. Against the romantics who longed for paradise lost he stressed that the 'common brotherhood of all men arrived fairly late on the scene and made such slow progress that only with Christianity was it generalised' (III: 287). So much for going back to nature!

Yet Hobbes was not the only culprit. One cannot, in fairness, accuse Hobbes of having established a new moral order. Indeed, it is possible that Hobbes merely sought to develop a solution to the circumstances in which he found himself. Further, Hobbes – unlike later utilitarians – did not believe that selfishness could have a positive spin-off. Indeed, Hobbes' conclusion was that only an autocratic despot would protect mankind from a 'Warre, and such a warre, as is of every man against every man' (Hobbes 1650: 64). In order to avoid this Hobbes would transfer all power to a 'mortal god', who would have the 'use of so much power and strength … conferred on him that by terror thereof he is inabled to forme the wills of all of them to peace at home, and mutuall ayd against their enemies abroad' (Hobbes 1650: 89–90).

Rousseau was not – to put it mildly – convinced by this argument. He wrote in *Du Contrat Social:*

> [Hobbes'] despot gives his subjects the assurance of civil tranquillity. Very well but what does it profit them, if those wars against other powers which

result from the despot's ambition, if his insatiable greed, and the oppressive demands of his administration, cause more desolation than civil strife would cause? What do people gain if their very condition of tranquillity is one of their hardships? There is peace in the dungeons but is that enough to make the dungeons desirable? (III: 355)

This was a question that Hobbes could not have answered. And yet Rousseau's attack on Hobbes did not have the intended effect of rendering the Englishman's approach to philosophy null and void. Hobbes differed from his followers. For while subsequent generations adopted his principle of human selfishness, they parted from Hobbes in assuming that selfishness could lead to a moral outcome. Faced with the altogether less horrifying spectre of emerging capitalism, a new generation of like-minded scholars (such as Adam Smith and Bernard Mandeville) concluded that selfishness, rather than leading to mutually assured destruction, would in fact result in untold economic benefits. Nowhere is this doctrine more clearly stated than in Smith's *An Inquiry into the Nature and Causes of the Wealth of Nations*, where the Scottish ideologue asserted:

> Give me that which I want, and you shall have this which you want, is the meaning of every offer; and it is in this manner that we obtain from one another the far greater part of those good offices which we stand in need of. It is not from the benevolence of the butcher, the brewer, or the baker, that we expect our dinner, but from their regard to their own interest. We address ourselves, not to their humanity but to their self-love. (Smith 1776: 26–7)

It is difficult to overestimate the importance and the implications of this statement for the subsequent development of ethical and economic theory. More than merely a statement of libertarian creed, Smith's credo provided a firm footing for economic thinking and political practice for generations of politicians. *Laissez-faire*, while seemingly immoral from a traditional Christian perspective (as well as from a Kantian one),[9] was perceived as the only efficient means of effectively allocating scarce resources. Having furnished a new outlook on human action, selfishness became the touchstone of practically all political thinkers, on the right as well as on the left. Even John Rawls, a thinker of the moderate left, felt compelled to base his theory of justice on the foundations of egotistical calculation (Rawls 1971: 85). This is not to say that it was all the result of the Enlightenment. It was a popular, if erroneous, assumption among many of the critics of modernity that Nietzsche's assassination of God was to blame for the moral decay and demise of ethics (Macintyre 1981). 'Without God, no morals', says one of the characters in Dostoevsky's *Demons*. Not really. In fact, the famed golden rule of 'do unto others as you would have them do unto you' (Matt. 7.12), which Hobbes cited (Hobbes 1651: 36) (!), was as much an example of consequentialism, as were later professions of this creed. While Christ may have intended it differently, the teaching of Hell and eternal damnation for those who failed to live up to the teachings of the Gospels became a morality based not on the 'purity of the heart', but on a calculation that one should behave in a fashion that would prevent you from eternal torment in Hell.[10] As Rousseau wrote to d'Offreville, '… in the system of religion, that is to say of punishments and rewards in the other life, you see that the interest of pleasing the Creator and judge of all our actions is so important as to outweigh the greatest evils' (Quoted in Gourevitch 1997b: 262). Christendom – in practice at least – had degenerated into consequentialism; a doctrine which was at odds with the teaching of Christ as perceived by Rousseau.

Rousseau lamented the demise of this system of morals and he never accepted this invisible hand. He wrote:

> All our writers regard the crowning achievement of our century's politics to be the sciences, the arts, the commerce, laws and all the other bonds which, by tightening the social ties among men through *self interest*, place them in a position of mutual dependence … and oblige everyone to contribute to everyone else's happiness in order to secure his own. These are certainly fine ideas, and they are presented in an attractive light. But when they are examined carefully and impartially, the advantages which they seem to hold out prove to be subject to a good many reservations. (II: 968)

Rousseau's moral philosophy, therefore, was not only a radical break with Hobbes, it was also a break with the perceived teachings of the Church(es). For Rousseau, the goal – however good – did not justify the means. In one of his *Frangments,* entitled *Des Moeurs,* he stated that 'for an action to be good [and just it must] not only be this in its ends but in all its relations' (III: 555) – clearly not a view that was compatible with the morals of selfishness. This view was later to become the central dogma in Immanuel Kant's moral philosophy. In *Foundations of the Metaphysics of Morals,* written in 1785, the German *Meister* famously noted that we should 'act so as to treat every rational being, whether in yourself, or in another, never as a means only, but also as ends' (quoted in Scruton 1981: 152). A moral individual is constrained by this 'Categorical imperative' not to bend others to his own purpose, not to enslave or exploit them but always to recognise their worth and dignity as fellow human beings created by God. The proto-Kantian approach (i.e. that other individuals must be goals rather than means) was perhaps most forcefully expressed in the moral creed of Rousseau's fictional heroine *Julie* in *La Nouvelle Heloïse*:[11] 'An individual', Rousseau lets her write, 'is too noble a being to be a mere *tool* for others. It is not to be used only for the needs of others without concern for its own wishes ... the aim is to be as good and as happy as possible' (II: 536, italics added). Individuals are ends not means. To base one's action on self-interest is to make that other individual into 'a mere tool for others', and hence unethical.

Having declared war on all the apostles of self-interest he sought to restate a true moral philosophy, based not on self-interest, but on a true concern for our fellow men. For, as he asked, why rely on moral philosophers 'when we can find [goodness] in our own hearts' (III: 30)? In contrast to most subsequent philosophers[12] – who sought to justify ethics in self-interest and who accepted this as the only credible axiom of ethical theory – Rousseau adopted not one but several axioms. Man was not the product of one passion or desire only. While accepting the existence of self-preservation (*amour de soi même*), he found Hobbes doctrine too restrictive as the latter had not distinguished between self-preservation and selfishness (*amour propre*). Yet these two drives of human action were not the only ones. There was a third; compassion – *pitié*. 'There is', wrote Rousseau,

> another principle, which has escaped Hobbes; which having been bestowed on mankind to moderate, on certain occasions, the impetuosity of egoism, or before its birth, the desire of self-preservation [*amour de soi même*], tempers it's ardour with which he pursues his own welfare, by innate repugnance of seeing his fellow creatures suffer ... I think I need not fear contradiction in holding men to be possessed of only one natural virtue, which could not be denied to him by even the most violent detractor of human nature; namely compassion [*pitié*]. (III: 154)[13]

A modern observer has summed it up as follows: 'against Hobbes and Locke and their followers, Rousseau insists that no amount of self interest ever leads to true concern for one's fellow as opposed to the fraudulent show of it. It is not merely that Enlightenment thought overestimates the possibilities of reason ... but that it underestimates those of sentiment' (Orwin 1997: 299). Rousseau himself wrote:

> The more complete our identification with the individual [who suffers] the greater our compassion with him. Even should it be true that pity is only a sentiment that puts us in the place of he who suffers – a sentiment that is obscure and strong in savage man but weakly developed in civilised man –

what would this idea matter to the truth of what I say, except give it more force? In fact, commiseration will be all the more energetic. (III: 155)

Libertarians may sing the praises of ethical egoism – and Rousseau was willing to concede that self-preservation was a laudable characteristic in man's constitution. Yet he pointed out that the insistence on merely one principle was not only unethical but also untenable. Again his tactic reveals that Rousseau was unconstrained by philosophical method and rational discourse. Robert Wokler has pointed to the post-modern traits in Rousseau's thought (Wokler 2001). Fittingly for a premature post-modernist, Rousseau used the language to show his point rather than to refute his opponents' philosophical arguments. 'In the most vigorous language', he writes in the *Origin of Language*, 'Everything is said symbolically, before one actually speaks … thus one speaks more effectively to the eye than to the ear' (V: 377) – a view which has been vindicated in the television era. True to his rhetorical observation he did not engage in a dialectical discourse with Hobbes and Mandeville, but rather refuted the doctrinaires of self-love, offering a description of:

> a man who, from a place of confinement, is compelled to behold a wild beast tear a child from the arms of its mother, grinding its tender limbs with its murderous teeth, and tearing its palpitating entrails with its claws. What horrid agitation must not the eye-witness of the scene experience, although he would not be personally concerned! What anxiety would he not suffer at not being able to give any assistance to the fainting mother and the dying infant?' (III: 154–5)

By presenting an appeal to the senses –and to the readers' natural compassion – Rousseau was able to pour scorn on Hobbes' purportedly realist account. That self-sacrifice could appeal to the heart was not a passing observation. Indeed, Juliet – his fictional heroine – sacrifices herself for her child in *La Nouvelle Heloïse* (Rousseau 1968: 401). All these actions are driven by *pitié*.[14]

But Rousseau, being a philosopher, did not stop at compassion. Especially in his *Essay on the Origin of Languages* he went a step further and sought to establish what we might call the transcendental conditions necessary for our compassion being stirred. As he wrote: 'Although compassion is native to the human heart, it would remain eternally quiescent unless it was activated by imagination (V: 395). It is, in other words, only by empathy – the ability to step into somebody else's shoes and then step out again, as Anna Freud has reportedly defined it[15] – that we can feel compassion. For it is only through this ability to get 'outside ourselves' we can 'suffer as much as we believe him [a fellow human being] to suffer' (V: 395).

'Don't tell it show it!' runs the maxim of television journalism. By appealing to our feelings (in his fictional as well as in his philosophical writings) Rousseau did not need to engage in a discussion about the truthfulness of Hobbes' description of man's motives as deriving from the sole concern of self-preservation. Rousseau *showed* us that Hobbes was wrong, he didn't argue his point. By presenting us with a case where self-sacrifice is – seemingly – the natural option, he had, in fact, rendered Hobbes' doctrine null and void, and had done so in a way, which was more understandable to the post-modernists of today than to the budding modernists of eighteenth-century France.

Hobbes was Rousseau's main target. Yet Rousseau was also profoundly inspired by the Englishman. Rather like Kant in relation to Hume, Hobbes awakened Rousseau from his dogmatic slumbers, and forced the latter to re-assess his own foundations by rethinking the origin of human society. So, while Rousseau was less of a 'scientist' than Hobbes, the former's analysis of the state of nature is much more realistic, and more explicitly built on empirical arguments than Hobbes'. Hobbes was a stringent writer displaying his Euclidean skills. Rousseau, no less stringent, was more of a Newtonian, preoccupied with empirical accuracy. Rather than merely stripping man of his social characteristics (as Hobbes did in *Leviathan*), Rousseau challenged Hobbes' notion that egotistical man was natural man, by outlining a hypothetical – though broadly empirically based – story of human evolution.[16] Foreshadowing later historicists, Rousseau emphasised that in the state of nature man was yet to develop the negative characteristics which Hobbes attributed to him. Primitive man, Rousseau argued, was also solitary man, and, as such, someone who had no conception of good and evil. 'Other men, it is true, were not to him what they now are to us; he had no greater intercourse with them than with other animals' (III: 166). The envy, contempt and vanity (*amour propre*) of Hobbes' state of nature were of a later date, and were only established once man entered into unequal societies, i.e. when strong individuals deceived others into believing that their might was right. It was only when this happened that man developed *amour propre*, which in turn poisoned the relationship between men. Rousseau often spoke of *l'error de Hobbes* (III: 298) – indeed Diderot even contrasted the two as antithetical in *L'Encycloplaedie*.

> The philosophy of M. Rousseau of Geneva is almost the opposite [*l'inverse*] of that of Hobbes. According to the philosopher of Geneva, the state of

nature is a state of peace, according to the philosopher of Malmesbury it is a state of war. (Diderot 1775: 240–1)

One could perhaps be forgiven for reaching the conclusion that Rousseau was a latterday advocate of an Aristotelian conception of man as a *zoon politicon*. He wasn't. Rousseau was rather the proponent of a third option – that is to say he borrowed from both. He rejected the rational choice position that man is an utility maximizer, yet he also (and perhaps more surprisingly) rejected Aristotle's position that 'the state is a creation of nature ... and man is by nature a political animal [*zoon politicon*]' (Aristotle 1984: 1253). Man, according to Rousseau, had to be taught to become a good citizen (IV: 600). Rousseau agreed with Hobbes that political society was not natural – as Aristotle had believed. Hence the establishment of society required conventions, which in turn required the consent of the governed. But is it possible to establish such a commonwealth? To answer this Rousseau found it necessary to inquire if it was possible to create a political order which was both just and compatible with man as he was created – as a naturally un-social (though not anti-social) individual (III: 351). In other words, would it be possible to 'combine what rights permits with what interest prescribes, so that justice and utility may not be disjoined', as he put it in *Du Contrat Social* (III: 351). His answer – in so far as it can be reduced to a single sentence – was that such a legitimate order was a 'form of association that will defend and protect the person and goods of each associate with full common force, and by means of which each, uniting with all, will be as free as before' (III: 360). Yet *Du Contrat Social* – the institutional framework – was not sufficient in itself. It could not stand alone. *Du Contrat Social*, therefore, did not present a rounded political theory of the best of all possible political worlds. It merely addressed the theoretical question of legitimacy. Rousseau was never in any doubt that institutions were but part of the equation, and possibly a minor one at that. 'Justice and utility', he believed, could only be reconciled through education (broadly defined) – i.e. through re-finding the natural goodness of man; his compassion for his fellow men (Melzer 1990). It has therefore been said that Rousseau elevated the status of *le bon sauvage*, and that he aspired to take men back to nature.[17]

There is an element of truth in this, though not in the banal sense often implied. Rousseau, for a start, was no fan of primitive man as he is found in tribes in remote areas of Asia, the Amazon and Africa. Indeed, he believed that these had already lost their innocence. The state of nature depicted by Hobbes, Rousseau conceded, was very much like the state 'reached by most savage nations known to us' (III: 170). Rousseau's natural man existed prior to the establishment of society – however primitive. Yet Rousseau, himself a *reveur solitaire*, was fascinated by and indeed drawn to this primitive existence – though he would vehemently claim the opposite. 'The good man orders himself in relation to the whole ... the wicked man orders the whole in relation to himself. The one makes himself the centre of all things; the other measures his radius and holds himself at the circumference' (IV: 356), he was later to write in *Emile*. But Rousseau did not always practice what he preached. The feeling of being alone and irresponsible (in the positive sense of the word, if there is such) attracted him. For primitive man, 'his soul ... is given to the single feeling of his own presence, without any idea of the future, however near it may be', wrote Rousseau (quoted in Froese 2001: 20). Some twenty years later he would define happiness in a very similar tone in *Reveries*: where he wrote:

> If there is a state where the soul can find a resting place secure enough to establish itself and concentrate its entire being there, with no need to remember the past or reach into the future, where time is nothing to it, where the present runs on indefinitely but this duration goes unnoticed, with no sign of the passing of time, and no other feeling of deprivation or enjoyment, pleasure or pain, desire or fear than the simple feeling of existence, a feeling that fills our soul entirely, as long as this state lasts, we can call ourselves happy. (I: 946)

The parallel is striking – though not necessarily intended.

Great works invite different interpretations – and often ones that are equally textually substantiated! A classic, it might be argued, invites different interpretations because the writer himself is wrestling with the deepest of questions. Rousseau is no exception, inspiring writers from Marxists, through liberals to conservatives. Can we take sides in the debate? Can we resolve the conflict between the warring fractions in the scramble for the intellectual corpse of the revered master?

The Left seems so far to have enjoyed a privileged position.[18] Indeed, one it seems to have fortified recently.[19] Andrew Levine, a proponent of the 'Jacobin' interpretation of Rousseau, even asserts that the latter not only was on the left and a revolutionary but that 'Marxian communism is an essentially Rousseauian idea' (Levine 1993: 159). Having described the blissful – though no longer obtainable – state of nature, and having singled out private property as the main culprit, we may conclude that Rousseau belongs to the radicals. Just witness the following outcry – which could serve as a battle cry of the anti-capitalists of the early 2000s:

The extreme inequality in our lifestyle: excessive idleness among some, excessive labour among others … are the fatal proofs that most of our ills are of our own making, and that we could have avoided nearly all of them by preserving the simple, regular, and solitary lifestyle prescribed to us by nature. (III: 138)

Add further Rousseau's famous observation that 'the first man, having enclosed a piece of ground, besought himself of saying this is mine, and found people simple enough to believe him', was an 'impostor', whose actions led to 'many crimes, wars, murders', and 'horrors and misfortunes'. Also his assertion that 'the fruit of the earth belongs to all of us and the earth itself to nobody' (III: 164), and the contours of a proto-communist are not far off. And, yet this interpretation leaves out main caveats and qualifications. Rousseau was not a revolutionary, still less a man who believed that anything could be solved by confiscating private property. Like Locke, he was a defender of private property.[20] Roughly at the same time as he wrote the just cited passage in *The Origin of Inequality*, he penned his essay on *Political Economy*, in which he boldly observed that 'the right of property is the most sacred of all rights of citizenship, and even more important in some respects than liberty itself because it affects the preservation of life' [*'le droit de propriété est le plus sacré de tous les droits des citoyens'*] (III: 263). Indeed, in *Emile* he even adopts the same justification of property rights as Locke had developed in his *Second Treatise* (Locke 1988: 99). Locke had argued that 'though the earth and all inferior creatures are common to all men, yet he has property in his own person … the labour of his body and the work of his hand, we may say are properly his … when a man has added something more than nature, the common mother of all had done … they [the things he has worked on] be his of right' (99).

Rousseau was under no illusion that property could be done away with. What he rejected was merely the accumulation of wealth. As a perceptive observer has put it; 'of the most salient aspects of Rousseau's critique of private property [was] the belief that ostentatious wealth poses the greatest danger to liberty' (Putterman 1999). True to his reverence for Christendom, Rousseau did not seek radical solutions, but merely stressed Christ's insistence that 'you cannot serve two masters; God and Mammon' (Matt. 6.24). He was adamant that 'it is one of the most important functions of government to prevent extreme inequality of fortunes' (III: 113), however, he was equally unequivocal that this goal could not be attained by 'taking away wealth from its possessors'. The negative consequences of excessive inequality – while generated by greed (and hence by private property) –

could not be cured by stripping man of one of his most fundamental rights. Rousseau, somewhat surprisingly for someone who has been canonised as the patron saint of the revolution, therefore rejected radical change, noting (rightly, it turned out) that 'revolutions hand themselves to seducers' (III: 113). Rather, he favoured education – a revolution of the mind – as the answer to the excesses of unbridled capitalism.

Rousseau was not a revolutionary, nor indeed was he a utopian. 'If we wish to form a durable establishment', he wrote in *Du Contrat Social*, 'let us not dream of making it eternal' ['*ne songeons donc point à rendre éternel*'] (III: 424). This anti-utopianism was a characteristic of his general outlook, and something we find in other parts of his oeuvre. In *Les Solitaires*, an unpublished sequel to *Emile*, the main character of the earlier work, while having received the most thorough education possible, still ended up leaving Juliet (his spouse) and failed to follow the teachings of his tutor. Rousseau was under no illusions that it was possible to establish a perfect society, yet he was a severe critic of bourgeois man all the same.

Small is beautiful: Rousseau's economic philosophy

So what did he want? Which alternative to capitalism on the one hand, and revolutionary change on the other, did he propose now that he rejected communism? A case can be made for the view that Rousseau developed the first 'Green' economic philosophy by synthesising the theories of the physiocrats and the mercantilists. Rousseau was no believer in free trade. Many of his doctrines may therefore appear strange in the current climate where the free market has become an article of faith. This, of course, does not make his analysis redundant. Rousseau was an acute observer on man's feeling of alienation – or anomie – in a society that had evolved in a way that was detrimental to his nature. Rousseau himself was not always sure that he had found a solution to the problem, nor did he necessarily seek one. He saw himself as an analyst rather than a problem solver. He expressed this view in one of his fragments, where he declared that 'I intend to attack more than establish truths' (quoted in Shklar 1969: 7) and in, the largely ignored, autobiographical essay *Mon Portrait* (I: 1120), where he stated: 'I am an observer, not a moralist. I am the botanist who describes the plant. It is for the physician to order its use.'[21] Unlike Marx – who remarked that philosophers, rather than interpreting the world, should change it – Rousseau was not a political activist. Yet, like Marx, he distinguished himself by making the right diagnosis of the plight of modern men and women. That both his and Marx's followers drew the wrong implications of this analysis is another story – and a tragic one at that, though perhaps one that could have been avoided had Rousseau's followers cared to consider the blueprint for reform Rousseau – despite his protestations – penned in the Autumn of his life.

Rousseau, while not opposed to private property, would have been opposed to most other doctrines of modern (capitalist) economics, especially international trade. His economic credo was founded upon a preference for economic self-sufficiency, agriculture and decentralised government. That is, an economic system that would be conducive to the simple life Rousseau cherished – and which always lies at the core of his thinking. It is somehow odd that these ideas have tended to be ignored by political and economic theorists as they are just as integrated into his philosophy as are his writings about the social contract. Bernard de Jouvenel has expressed it thus: 'his [Rousseau's] influence on our ideas presents a paradox. For the political ideas of *Du Contrat Social* have profoundly affected us, but the social ideas, which have a larger place in the work of Rousseau, have not done so at all' (de Jouvenel 1965: 18). Or perhaps it was Jouvenel who was in the wrong. For while Rousseau may not have much in common with the free marketers of the early twenty-first century, his writings seem rather closer to the modern environmentalist economists than is commonly recognised.[22]

In the history of economics Rousseau may appear as a marginal figure (Putterman 1999; Fridén 1998). That is not how it always was. Bertil Fridén, in an insightful study, offers this interesting observation:

> The spot was not always marginal. In the enlightened salons of Paris during the decades just before the fall of the *Ancien Regime*, Rousseau's economic philosophy was evidently a hot topic. The editors of the great *Encyclopédie* selected Rousseau to write the article on political economy in Tome V. They selected him, not Quesnay, Mirabeau, Turgot, Condorcet or Diderot himself.
> (Fridén 1998: 13)

The economic thinking of his time was dominated by two schools; the physiocrats and the mercantilists. The former favoured agricultural production and *laissez-faire* economics, the latter favoured non-agricultural production and opposed free trade.

Physiocracy has been described as a 'form of agrarian capitalism' (Fermon 1997: 136). The term was coined by Pierre Samuel du Pont de Nemours, in 1767, to describe Quesnay's economic doctrine. Quesnay rejected artisan and proto-industrial forms of production. Where mercantilists in both Britain and France held that wealth was created by the process of exchange – which could be boasted by manufacturers – the physiocratrats held that agriculture was the best means of generating prosperity. 'The sovereign', wrote Quesnay, 'should not lose sight of the fact that the earth is the unique source of wealth, and that it is agriculture which causes it to multiply' (Quesnay quoted in Fermon 1997: 137).[23]

Subsequent thinkers borrowed from both these schools. Adam Smith, the most prominent, combined the physiocrats' zeal for free trade with the mercantilists' enthusiasm for non-agricultural production. Rousseau did the opposite. He adopted the physiocrats' preference for agricultural production – but sided with the mercantilists on the matter of free trade. It was, historically speaking, the former view that initially won the day. Smith's doctrine became the touchstone of the science of economics, Rousseau's view sank into oblivion. (At least until he was resurrected by present-day environmentalists.)

While his reputation declined, it seems that elements of his thinking can be found in the doctrine that 'small is beautiful'. He questioned the wisdom of free trade and liberalism, as well as attacking consumerism, materialism, and defending small-scale production. Rousseau's position on trade and commerce was as harsh as it was unequivocal; 'the financial systems are modern', noted the conservative Rousseau, and continued, 'I can see nothing good or great coming out of them' (III: 1004). Money, for Rousseau, could never be but a means to an end (III: 519). The objection to finance capitalism was not, as discussed in the previous chapter, a sign of any fundamental objection to the principle of private property. What Rousseau objected to was merely the degenerated form of a liberal economy. He believed that an economic system based solely on egotistical rationalism would yield increased inequalities, and this he resented above all; 'it is', he wrote in *Discourse sur l'inégalité*, 'contrary to the law of nature that the privileged few should shower themselves in superfluities, while the starving multitudes are in want of the bare necessities of life' (III: 194).

His remedy for this inequality was the establishment of economically self-sufficient units, united in a federal system (a blueprint of this was developed in *Projet du Corse*). But there was more to his economic thinking than just this. Unlike modern economists, who pay relatively little attention to political matters, Rousseau sought to combine his thinking on economic matters with his political outlook. An adherent to a realist interpretation of international affairs (Waltz 1959) – i.e. as someone who saw international politics as the naked struggle for power – he found that reliance on free trade was both unwise and utopian – as well as it would have negative implications within societies (such as growing inequality). 'The only means to maintain a nation in independence from others is agriculture. Had you all riches of the world but nothing with which to nourish yourself, you would depend on others' (III: 903). There are several interesting aspects of this view, not least that Rousseau also expresses an ecological awareness in addition to his political concerns. When advising the Corsicans to adopt an economic system based on agriculture he is aware that the natural resources are scarce:

> [T]he island abounds with wood suited for building material as well as for fuel yet one should not *exhaust this abundance* and leave the usage and cutting to the proprietors. In the same measure as the population grows and the cultivation multiplies *a rapid devastation of the woods* will take place. (III: 926, italics added)

The proto-ecologist Rousseau, therefore, urged that it was 'necessary to establish in good time a policy for the forests, and to regulate the cuttings in such a way that it equals consumption' (III: 926). While Rousseau thus indicated an awareness of ecological thoughts – an awareness which is truly historically unique – he was not an ecologist. Deforestation and independence were not the only reasons for advocating self-sufficiency. An economic system based on agriculture would also be consistent with his militant opposition against luxuries (a theme that formed a large part of the argument in *Discourse sur les sciences et les arts*).[24] In 1750 he had argued that 'money though it buys everything else, cannot buy morals and citizens' (III: 20). In order to acquire the latter two things (which were indispensable in a viable republic), he urged the adoption of a system which would: 'Get the people to spread over the surface of the territory, get them to stay there, to cultivate the love for rural life and work connected with it, and so find the necessities and satisfaction of life that they don't want to leave it' (III: 904). For in addition to preventing luxury this system would also ensure that 'the whole world lives and nobody enriches himself' (904).

It has been argued that *all* of Rousseau's subsequent ideas were contained in *On Political Economy*. One might equally argue that all his mature thoughts reached their zenith in *Projet du Corse*, where he combined his Spartan romance for rural austerity, a concern for the poor, a realist understanding of international relations – and an understanding of the necessity of nation building and maintaining a viable polity. In advocating this system Rousseau parted company with the emerging liberal tradition for whom nationalism, ecologism and realist politics are obstacles for creating the optimal conditions for the invisible hand. It is fair to say that Adam Smith won the argument – or at least the first round. Yet there are perhaps some who would argue that Rousseau might be vindicated by history. The classical liberals' scarce concern for the environment and natural resources, along with their failure to acknowledge that man does *not* live of material wealth alone is perhaps – it is still too early to tell – an indication that Rousseau's economic thinking is less anachronistic than it first appears. Bernard de Jouvenel found that Rousseau's thoughts on these matters had descended into oblivion. Another, more recent commentator has reached a different conclusion: 'what', asks Pierre Hassner, 'would have been Rousseau's response to the current situation'? (Hassner 1997: 215). Hassner provided this answer: 'he would have condemned, deplored or derided the ideological victory of free trade, and welcomed resistance to it. He would have sided with American unionists against NAFTA, with French farmers against GATT, with Third World radicals and with the *dependencia* school … and against unequal exchange and the imperialism of free-trade' (216).

A reactionary republican: Rousseau and Burke

'Nations stumble upon establishments, which are indeed the result of human action but not the result of human design' (Fergusson 1767: 187). Thus wrote Adam Fergusson, a prominent thinker of the Scottish Enlightenment, and – alongside Edmund Burke, David Hume, and Josiah Tucker – a proponent of the belief that spontaneous, unplanned action often creates greater things than individual minds can comprehend. 'The forms of societies', continued Fergusson, 'are derived from an obscure and distant origin: they arise long before the date of philosophy, from instincts, not from the speculations of man … we ascribe to a previous design, what became known only by experience, what no human wisdom could foresee, and what without the concurring humour and disposition of age, no authority could enable an individual to execute' (187). This scepticism in the powers of human reason might seem misplaced in the age of rationalism. This anti-constructivist conception of society as something that has evolved through what Hayek was later to call 'spontaneous action', was rejected by – and largely written in opposition to – a different conception of society, which we might call (for want of a better expression), constructivist. René Descartes, in *Discourse on Method*, was a proponent of the constructivist view. He argued that 'there is seldom so much perfection in works composed of many separate parts, upon which different hands had been employed, as in those composed by a single master'. And he went on to say, 'the past pre-eminence of Sparta was not due to the pre-eminence of each of its laws in particular ... but to the circumstance that, originated by a single individual, they all tended to a single end' (Descartes 1950: 60). As in epistemology, so too in practical philosophy, Descartes, the rationalist, was opposed to Hume, the empiricist. Where the Frenchman was a constructivist the Scot was not. The latter wrote:

> It is not with forms of government as with other contrivances where an old engine may be rejected, if we can discover another more accurate and commodious, or where trials may safely be made, even though the success be doubtful. An established government has an indefinite advantage, by that very circumstance of being established; the bulk of mankind being governed by authority not reason ... To temper, therefore, in this affair, or try experiments merely upon credit of supposed argument and philosophy, can never be part of a wise magistrate. (Hume 1985: 512)

As would be expected, historians of the ideas have rightly seen traces of this dichotomy throughout the history of Western political thought. Plato, Augustin, Descartes, Hobbes, di Campanella, Voltaire, Marx and Comte were – in various degrees – 'constructivists', whereas Aristotle, Cicero, Locke, Burke and Hume could be categorised in the opposite camp. Rousseau has hitherto been unequivocally placed among the former. Hayek, to mention but one writer, thus sees a chain of 'design theories of social institutions, from Descartes through Rousseau and the French Revolution down to what is still a characteristic attitude of the engineers to social problems' (Hayek 1948: 10). Hayek was not the only one to get this wrong. McManner's comment that the philosophy of Rousseau 'is the work of a revolutionary condemning all existing institutions' (McManner 1972: 305), is another example of this fallacy. In fact, Rousseau argued that 'all the laws of Europe were made little by little, by bits and pieces, an abuse appeared and a law was made to deal with it' (III: 975). Hayek was not alone in thinking that Rousseau was a constructivist. Edmund Burke's case against Rousseau – and the French Revolution – was, above all, based on what he saw as the latter's constructivist approach. It is, however, questionable if Burke in reality held views that differed significantly from those propagated by Rousseau. As Annie Marion Osborn has found in her *Rousseau and Burke*: 'When Edmund Burke thundered forth his vitriolic denunciations of Rousseau, he had no conception of the fact that they were both dreaming of a better society in which men would be free and would be willing to assume the responsibilities of citizenship in a state dedicated to liberty' (Osborn 1940: 238). 'We are not', wrote Burke in *Reflections on the Revolution in France*, 'the converts of Rousseau, we are not the disciples of Voltaire ... atheists are not our preachers' (Burke 1790: 282). Burke might be forgiven for his rejection of Rousseau. Indeed, the latter's thinking was often singled out as a scapegoat among contemporary writers – and was commonly associated with Voltaire. William Blake, for instance, wrote in his *Notebook:*

> Mock, mock Voltaire, Rousseau
> Mock, mock on 'tis all in vain
> You throw the sand against the wind
> And the wind throws it back again

(Blake 1979: 184)

Burke (and Blake, it seems) used Rousseau as a convenient political scapegoat. Burke's charge would, perhaps, have been true had he focused solely on Voltaire, who – unlike Rousseau – advocated revolutionary change. Or, as he bluntly put it in his *Dictionaire Philosophique*, 'if you want good laws, burn those you have and make yourself new ones' (Voltaire, n.d., 32). Yet Burke was wrong to lay all the blame at Voltaire. Helvétius held the same views. Writing with revolutionary fervour, he noted that the only means of improving society was to reject 'the stupid veneration for old laws and customs' (Helvétius 1973: 144). Rousseau never wrote anything to this effect.

It is therefore slightly puzzling why Burke misrepresented Rousseau, as the British MP-cum-thinker had been aware of the Swiss writer for decades and had read his works. Burke's opposition to Rousseau was not confined to the years around the French Revolution. He had written a sharply critical review of Rousseau's *Letter to d'Alembert* in the *Annual Register* for 1759 and a similarly critical review of *Emile* for the same publication in 1762. His dislike of the Genevan – which was shared by many of his generation (for example Samuel Johnson)[25] – was merely systematised after the Revolution. The thrust, however, was the same. Burke assumed, almost a priori, that the Revolution's excesses were to be a direct consequence of Rousseau's teachings. Interestingly Burke *never* quoted Rousseau.

It has been asserted that Rousseau's theory could be seen as an alternative to the ideal of limited government (Barber 1988). While Rousseau did not advocate a Hayekean theory (Hayek 1960), let alone a Nozickean doctrine of the Minimal state (Nozick 1973), he was adamant that the magistrates should pass as few laws as possible, as legislation potentially undermined already existing institutions, which have proven their worth in the course of time. The magistrates did not – and could not – know the consequences of their enactments. Their predictions as to the consequences of their laws could prove to be flawed, which could result in dire consequences. Rousseau thus urged legislative caution. While 'the magistrates' ought to have a monopoly of proposing legislation, they should only use 'this right', he wrote in *Discourse sur l'inégalité*,

> with so much caution ... that before the constitution could be upset by them, there might be time enough for all to be convinced ... by accustoming themselves to neglect ancient customs under the pretext of improvements states often introduce greater evils than they endeavour to remove. (III: 114)

Arguably a view which resembled Burke's view in *Reflections on the Revolution in France* – which has traditionally been described as the quintessential statement of the Tory doctrine of gradual reform. Burke wrote, in rejection of the 'violent haste' of the French revolutionaries:

> At once to preserve and to reform is quite another thing. When the useful parts of an old establishment are kept and what is superadded is to be fitted to what is retained ... Such a mode of reforming possibly might take up many years. Without question in mind, and it ought. It is one of the excellencies of a method in which time is among the assistants, that its operation is slow, and in some cases almost imperceptible. (Burke 1986: 280)

Rousseau could not have agreed more. Almost echoing his foremost critic, Rousseau concurred, 'men soon learn to despise laws which they see daily altered (III: 114). This was not a mere passing *idée fix*, indeed, in *Considérations sur la gouvernement du Polonge*, written seventeen years later, he again stressed: 'let us never lose sight of the important maxim; do not change anything, add nothing, subtract nothing, unless you have to' (III: 975). Again – like Burke – Rousseau's justification for this conservatism – was a profound scepticism with the practical usefulness of political science. In *Lettre à Mirabeau*, a physiocrat, Rousseau noted that the art of government is nothing but 'a science of combinations, applications, and exceptions' (Quoted in Gourevitch 1997b, 269). An approach to government, which, if anything, was consistent with Burke's view that the 'science of constructing a commonwealth ... is like every other experimental science, not to be taught a priori. Nor is it a short experience' (Burke 1986: 442). Burke, who never missed an opportunity to excoriate Rousseau, presumably, was unaware of this. Perhaps Burke would – had he read Rousseau's entire output – have hailed him as a great Tory? It seems that the probability of this would have increased even further had Burke paid attention to Rousseau's denunciation of violent change, which he believed would lead to despotism:

> If they [the people] attempt to shake off the yoke will still more estrange themselves from freedom, as, by mistaking for it an unbridled licence to which it is diametrically opposed, they nearly always manage, by their resolutions, to hand themselves over to seducers, who only make their chains heavier than before. (III: 113)

Burke could not have put it better. But there are more similarities. Burke noted in *Reflections* that 'our passions instruct our reasons' (Burke 1986: 442); Rousseau, in a similar way, found, in *The Origin of Language*, that 'feelings speak before reason' (V: 417). This scepticism as regards rationalism – and faith in tradition – is what places the two adversaries on the same side in the battle. Other philosophers maintained that it was possible, once we have fathomed what Adam Smith called 'the secrets of social astronomy' (Smith 1937: 200) – to engineer society in accordance with our wishes. These constructivist philosophers strove to become for the political sciences what Newton had been for the physical sciences. Like Burke, Rousseau, true to his distrust of reason, rejected this constructivist view. Further, he also held it impossible that man could ever achieve an understanding of society that would enable him to legislate for a perfect society. Foreshadowing a critique later to be developed by the philosophers of the Scottish Enlightenment, Burke and Hayek (see Hayek 1948 for an overview), Rousseau stressed that it would be impossible to know all the consequences of legislative action. Legislation was not a panacea, as believed by revolutionaries, and fellow-travellers such as Jeremy Bentham.

Caution was the common denominator in the philosophies presented by Burke and Rousseau. This relationship is rarely noted though difficult to ignore. Sceptics, who may still regard Rousseau as a revolutionary (and Burke's antithesis), are challenged to explain this rejection of Abbé de Saint-Pierre's utopian proposal for a European superstate:

> one must begin by destroying everything [*tous ce qui existe*] to give the government the form imagined by Abbe de Saint-Pierre, and no one knows how dangerous it is to create a moment of anarchy and crisis which necessarily must precede the establishment of new institutions in large states … who can hold back [*retenir*] the earthquake, or foresee all the effects it will have. While this plan has incontestable benefits, who will take responsibility for changing established norms and old customs, which it has taken more than 1300 years to establish? (III: 637–8)

It is the cruel irony of history that the only philosopher in the eighteenth century who predicted the dire consequences of violent revolutions become associated – through no fault of his own – as the patron saint of the French Revolution, and through this with all subsequent violent overthrows of established political orders.

Notes

1 See, for example, Christopher Ricks, *Keats and Embarrassment* (Clarendon Press: Oxford, 1974), p. 178.

2 On Voltaire see John Gray, *Voltaire* (Routledge: London, 1988).

3 On Rousseau and Weber see J.G. Merquior, *Rousseau and Weber: Two Studies in the Theory of Legitimacy* (London: Routledge and Kegan Paul, 1980).

4 See Pierre Burgelin, *La philosophie de l'existence de J.-J. Rousseau* (Paris: Vrin, 1952) and Michel Coz and François Jacob (eds), *Rêveries sans fin: autour des 'Rêveries du promeneur solitaire'* (Orléans: Paradigme, 1997).

5 On the unfulfilled promises of the enlightenment see John Grey, *Enlightenment's Wake. Politics and Culture at the Close of the Modern Age* (Routledge, London, 1995).

6 Economists have shown that when people have imperfect knowledge the invisible-hand theory does not work. For a formal argument see J.E. Stiglitz (1986), 'Externalities in Economics with Imperfect Information and Incomplete Markets', in *Quarterly Journal of Economics*, vol. 101, no. 2, pp. 229–64.

7 Cited from The World Bank, *Global Economic Prospects and Developing Countries* (Washington DC: The World Bank, 2000), p. 29.

8 For a thorough study of Helvétius' influence upon Bentham and Marx see Irwing Horowitz's essay 'Helvétius, Bentham and Marx' (Horowitz 1954: 170).

9 There is considerable literature on Rousseau and Kant. For a recent, balanced, account see Richard L. Velkley, *Freedom and the End of Reason* (Chicago: University of Chicago Press, 1999).

10 In *not* seeking divine justification for moral judgements Rousseau is probably closer to Iris Murdoch. See Murdoch, *The Sovereignty of the Good* (Oxford: Oxford University Press, 2000).

11 The relationship between Rousseau's own thoughts and those of his fictional characters is widely discussed, as is his novel. For a thorough understanding the reader might consult: Anne Tilleul, *La vertu du beau: essai sur 'La nouvelle Héloïse'* (Montréal: Humanitas, 1989); Byron R. Wells, *Clarissa and La nouvelle Héloïse: dialectics of struggle with self and others* (Ravenna: Longo, 1985); Claude Labrosse, *Lire au XVIIIe siècle: 'La nouvelle Héloïse' et ses lecteurs* (Lyon: Presses Universitaires de Lyon, 1985); Michel Launay *et al.*, *Jean-Jacques*

Rousseau et son temps: politique et littérature au XVIIIe siècle (Paris: Nizet, 1969); Jean-Louis Lecercle, *Rousseau et l'art du roman* (Paris: Armand Colin, 1969).

12 In fact Adam Smith concurred with him. In the *Theory of Moral Sentiments* he departed from the axiom of rational self-interest. Smith himself wrote in *The Theory of Moral Sentiments*: 'man ... ought to regard himself, not as something separated and detached, but as a citizen of the world, a member of the vast commonwealth of nature ... To the interest of this great community, he ought at all times to be willing that his own little interest should be sacrificed' (Smith cited in Amartya Sen, *On Ethics and Economics* (Oxford: Blackwell, 1988), pp. 22–3.

13 See I. Fetscher, *Rousseaus politische Philosophie* (Neuwied: Hermann Luchterhand, 1960).

14 This concept is mainly developed in the *Discourse sur l'inégalité* and in *Essay on the Origin of Languages*. It should be noted here that some commentaries have identified slight differences in the way Rousseau uses the term in the two works. Fetcher's illuminating *Rousseaus politische Philosophie* was seminal in focusing attention on this problem, even before French scholars began writing about it.

15 I have been unable to trace this reference, and cannot therefore verify it.

16 It is a cruel irony that Rousseau, the thinker most opposed to the godlessness of modernity, thus became one of the first thinkers to propose an evolutionary theory (roughly one hundred years before Charles Darwin). Rousseau's writing on the subject was greatly inspired by Buffon's, whose *Histoire naturelle* began to appear in 1749. The *Discourse sur l'inégalité* was in large measure based on Buffon's system and account of human history (III: 195–6).

17 See, for example, Jacques Derrida in *On Grammatology*: 'according to Rousseau ... evil is exterior to nature, to what by nature is innocent and good'. Derrida, *Of Grammatology* (Baltimore: Johns Hopkins University Press, 1976), p. 145.

18 See, for example, Louis Althusser, 'Sur le Contrat Social (les décalages)', in *Cahiers pour l'analyse*, 1970, vol. 8, pp. 5–42, and Michel Launay, *Jean-Jacques Rousseau écrivain politique 1712–1762* (Paris et Genève: Slatkine, 1989).

19 Marx himself occasionally quoted Rousseau – though not always approvingly. He criticised the German Social Democrats' Gotha Programme with the words 'In short one could just as well have copied the whole of Rousseau', quoted in Christopher Brooke, 'Rousseau's political Philosophy', in Patrick Riley, *The Cambridge Campanion to Rousseau* (Cambridge: Cambridge University Press, 2001). For a more thorough discussion of Marx and Rousseau see Galvano della Volpe (1970), 'The Marxist Critique of Rousseau', *New Left Review*, vol. 59.

20 As N.J.H. Dent has pointed out, Rousseau *never* advocated the abolition of private property. Dent, *A Rousseau dictionary* (Oxford: Blackwell, 1992). On

this subject see also A. Cobban, *Rousseau and the Modern State* (London: Allen & Unwin, 1934), p. 131.

21 As we are unlikely to come back to this point later, it ought to be noted that Rousseau was a botanist too. Indeed he was a rather accomplished one at that. He drafted long letters on botanical topics between 1771 and 1773. While he was engaged in the meticulous study of the systematisation of plants (IV: 1220) he evidently – and as expected – preferred to study plants as a kind of worshipping of nature. The Seventh Walk of the *Reveries* is typical, and hence worth quoting at some length: 'I shall remember all my life a botanical expedition I once made on the slopes of Robeila, a mountain belonging to Justice Clerc [in the region of Môtiers, where Rousseau lived from 1763–65]. I was alone, I made far into the crevices of the rocks, and going from thicket to thicket and rock to rock I finally reached a corner so deeply hidden away that I do not think I have ever seen a wilder spot: black fir trees were mingled and intertwined with gigantic beeches, several of which had fallen with age ... Here I found seven-leaved coral-wort, cyclamen, *nidus avis*, the large *laserpitium* and a few other plants which occupied and delighted me for some time, but gradually succumbing to the powerful impression of my surroundings, I forgot about botany and plants and sat down on pillows of *lycopodium* and mosses, and began dreaming to my heart's content, imagining that I was in a sanctuary unknown to the whole universe' (I: 1068–9).

22 See M. Smith, 'The State of Nature: The Political Philosophy of Primitivism and the Culture of Contamination', in *Environmental Values*, November 2002, vol. 11, no. 4, pp. 407–25 (p. 19).

23 On Rousseau's relationship with the physiocrats see: Jean Satra, 'Jean-Jacques Rousseau, économiste et l'école physiocratique', in Robert Thierry (ed.) *Jean-Jacques Rousseau, Politique et Nation* (Paris: Honoré Champion, 2001).

24 He elaborated on this point in the fragment *Le Luxe, le Commerce et les Arts* (III: 516–24).

25 See the exchange with Boswell on the subject of Rousseau in James Boswell, *The Life of Johnson LLD* (London: John Murray, 1831), vol. II, pp. 224–8.

3

Checks, balances and popular participation:
Rousseau as a constitutionalist

The liberty of the whole of humanity did not justify the shedding of blood
of a single man. (Jean-Jacques Rousseau, L. 5450)

Rousseau's denunciation of violence as a means to an end, in his letter to
the Countess of Wartesleben, is in stark contrast to the picture painted of
him by his adversaries (see the previous chapter). While it is generally
acknowledged that J.L. Talmon (1952) was unduly one-sided (Hampsher-
Monk 1995) when accusing Rousseau's 'Jacobin' philosophy for requiring
'intimidation [and] election tricks', it is still widely asserted that Rousseau
– through guilt of association – can be condemned and convicted for
promoting a doctrine of the 'general will' which in 'itself poses a threat to
individuals who might find themselves at odds with that [general] will'
(Barry 1995: 51). Even writers sympathetic to Rousseau admit that his
allegedly totalitarian theory (Barker 1948) 'required heavy doses of civic
education' (Shklar 1988: 267); not exactly a ringing endorsement at a time
when liberalism (in different guises) has become all but an article of faith.
It is debatable if this charge of totalitarianism is justified, and, indeed,
plausible. Totalitarianism is characterised by a deliberate attempt to change
people to fit a political system or a historical development (Barber 1987:
525).[1] Proponents of the thesis that Rousseau was a totalitarian seem to
have overlooked that he explicitly set out to inquire 'whether in civil order
there can be some legitimate and sure rule of administration, taking men
as they are' ('*tels qu'ils sont*') (III: 351).

Some writers have sought to rescue Rousseau from the charge of
authoritarianism by pointing to the allegedly metaphorical intentions of
his writings (see Putterman 2001 for a review). Miller – in an often quoted
study – argues that Rousseau deliberately 'charged the uncertain region
between dream and reality, between impossible ideals and remote

possibilities ... the treacheries of tempting them in practice, to travel the path indicated by his thinking had virtually convinced him to abandon the attempt' (Miller 1984: 131). It has occasionally been suggested that Rousseau imagined himself as legislator (Fralin 1978). 'In fact', writes Judith Shklar with characteristic assertiveness, 'he thought nothing of the sort ...no one had a clearer view of the differences between the life of action and the life of observation, and he knew himself to be capable only of the latter' (Shklar 1969: 133).

Whether Rousseau entertained the thought of becoming a latter-day Solon is a contentious question, unlikely ever to be resolved.[2] What seems uncontentious, however, is that he championed a doctrine of 'positive liberty' (Berlin 1969: 131). It would be sheer folly to contend that Rousseau was a theorist of 'negative liberty'. Rousseau was, as Berlin noted, at pains to show that liberty 'entails not simply the absence of frustration but also the absence of obstacles to possible choices' (Berlin 1969: xxxix). Some have seen this as proof of his totalitarian leanings.

This adherence to positive liberty does not automatically relegate him to the league of authoritarians – although some have reached this conclusion (Riker 1982: 9). Other thinkers with similarly soft spots for positive liberty, for example Mill, have escaped this charge (Thompson 1976: 136). Rousseau's *Wirkungsgeschichte* has been less fortunate (Cobban 1968 for an overview). Louis Sebastien Mercier singled him out as one of the 'first authors of the revolution' ('*l'un des premiers auteurs de la révolution*') (Mercier 1791; see also Swenson 1999), and he has often been quoted, for example by Burke (1791) and Constant (1818), as a 'Jacobin', and as someone who 'furnished deadly pretexts for more than one tyranny' (Constant 1988: 317). That Robbespierre himself singled him out as the chief ideologue of the terror regime has done his reputation few favours (Barny 1986: 120).

The main charge is that he, through his doctrine of the General Will, through his allegedly uncritical advocacy of plebiscitary democracy, and through his alleged opposition to checks and balances, has become the antithesis of constitutional democracy. The case for the prosecution has been stated by J.L. Talmon, who finds that Rousseau 'puts the people in the place of the physiocratic despot' (Talmon 1952: 45). Moreover, Talmon believed that 'at the very foundation of the principle of direct and indivisible democracy ... there is the implication of dictatorship' (46).

There are, however, scholars who – with ample textual evidence – have pointed out that Rousseau's positive concept of liberty, in general, and his theory of popular participation in particular, does not make him a totalitarian (Leigh 1964).[3] But it is as if his advocates, in their eagerness to defend him, trade in that very multiplicity of readings and meanings which have earned him a position in the canon of Western thought.

Rousseau is a thinker who invites many different interpretations. Such is the fate of the genius (Strong 1994: 2). A thinker with a taste for paradoxes, he has inspired conservatives (Bloom 1960) as well as Marxists (Levine 1993) and feminists (Fernon 1997) alike (Gourevitch 1998). Far from claiming that there is but one true interpretation, one can read Rousseau's political theory as – among other things – a contribution to what we, for want of a better expression, may call 'constitutionalism', i.e. the doctrine which emphasises the necessity of checks and balances on power. First, however, an overview of the debate as it has evolved through the different epochs of political history.

Absolutism and constitutionalism

Lord Acton is often cited for the dictum 'power corrupts – and absolute power corrupts absolutely' (Letter to Bishop Mandell Creighton). It followed from this – at least according to Acton – that power had to be checked and restricted, for example through constitutional courts, a royal veto, or powerful second chambers. We will call this view 'constitutionalism'. Yet this school is not unopposed. Invoking a perhaps simplistic dichotomy *à la* Isaiah Berlin (1953; 1969), we may draw a distinction between two fundamental political traditions in Western political thought; the *absolutists*, who, for fear of political chaos, believe that all power should be united in one individual or group of individuals, and the *constitutionalists*, who believe that all power should be checked, lest the rulers arrogate to themselves powers to which they are not entitled. Among the former we may cite Plato, Hobbes, Jean Bodin, Robert Filmer, Karl Marx, Carl Schmidt and Lenin. Among the latter we may cite Aristotle, Cicero, Locke, Montesquieu, Madison, Hayek and possibly even Machiavelli (McCormick 2001: 297).

Like all dichotomies this one stretches reality, and may become inaccurate and even absurd when applied too rigorously. However, as a heuristic device it may serve a purpose, namely by identifying the common denominators which we might otherwise overlook. Moreover, this distinction can even be found in the empirical literature (Ertmann 1997), as well as theorists have used the distinction for hundreds of years. Thus in 1476 the English statesman Sir John Fortescue distinguished, in his tract *The Governance of England: Otherwise called the Difference between*

Absolute and Limited Monarchy, between absolutist states in which the King 'mey rule his people bi suche lawes as he makyth hym self' and those countries (the constitutional ones) in which the King 'may not rule his people bi other laws than such as thai assenten unto' (Fortescue 1885: 109).[4]

These traditions are diverse. The absolutists believe that the 'legislator' should have absolute and unlimited power – in order that legislation can be based on a single, consistent and rational basis. Yet, there is considerable disagreement as to who the ruler should be; Lenin proposed that it should be the vanguard of 'the party', in *What is to be Done*; Plato made a case for philosopher kings in the *Republic* (Plato 1974: 499) – though he changed his mind in νομοι (*The Laws*) (Plato 1975: 676–93); and Hobbes – perhaps the foremost of the modern absolutists – made a case for the total transfer of powers to the *Leviathan*.[5] The latter writes, 'Sovereign power ought in all commonwealths to be absolute' (1973: 136). It is not difficult to point out the differences among these thinkers. What unites them, however, is that they all, in different ways and for different reasons, believed and contended that legislation – lest it should become spasmodic and irregular – should be undertaken on the basis of one belief system, namely that which represented the truth, reflected the Platonic forms (*eidos*), or was consistent with the 'laws of motion of society' (Marx 1978: 447). This view was lucidly expressed by Arthur Schoppenhauer – not normally considered a political thinker – in his *The World as Will and Representation*:

> The great value of monarchy seems to me to lie in the fact that because men remain men, one must be placed so high, and be given so much power, wealth and security, and absolute inviolability that for him there is nothing left to desire, to hope or to fear. (Schoppenhauer 1958: 595)

It has often been argued that Rousseau subscribed to this view (Popper 1945). Hayek thus wrote that Rousseau believed that 'democracy necessarily means unlimited power of the majority' (Hayek 1978: 6).[6] We shall return to this in a moment.

The constitutional tradition – no less diverse than the absolutist school – is based on the common assumption that no group or individual should have absolute power. This view seems – with the unavoidable exceptions – to be grounded in the epistemological assumption that all human knowledge is fallible.[7] As no one has access to the truth – in the essentialist meaning of the term[8] – no one individual or group should be entrusted with absolute power. The power should be checked, for example through institutions which enable the rulers to think again. Saul Levmore has summed up this view in the phrase 'two decisions are better than one' (Levmore 1992). James Madison, one of the best-known constitutionalists, famously summed up the view that central power be moderated by checks and balances, in *Federalist Paper No.51*. The basic reasoning was that the creation of a large number of independent public institutions which would, could – and should – veto politicians:

> [T]he great security against gradual concentration of several powers in some departments consists in giving to those who administer each department the necessary constitutional means and personal motives to resist encroachments of others. Ambition must be made to counteract ambition. (Madison in Hamilton *et al.* 1961: 319)

The different 'players' in the political game act as brakes. Rousseau did not follow Madison all the way. He never believed – as did Smith and Madison – that selfishness alone could be turned into a force for good. But he realised that institutions could play a part in shaping a just republic.

It follows, therefore, that the enactment of legislation should be made conditional upon concurrent endorsements of at least two distinct political institutions, such as parliament and the executive, both chambers in a bi-cameral legislature, etc. To understand this tradition we must temporarily break off the narrative to take a look at its history – or rather its genealogy.

The genealogy of constitutionalism

It has been asserted – probably correctly – that constitutionalism was originally invented by (or entrusted upon) the Israelites. The law given to Moses by the Lord (Exodus 20), was the birth of constitutionalism (Finer 1997). For the first time in history, a polity established the principle that the power of the king, or ruler, was restricted by a higher law. As a political historian has observed 'the monarch [was] bound by an explicit and written law code imposed upon him, coequally with his subjects, *from the outside*' (Finer 1997: 239, italics in the original). In introducing this doctrine, the Jews established, before anyone else – and at a time when unrestricted despotism was the order of the day – the concept of the 'rule of law', or the *Rechtsstaat*. Yet it does not follow from this that the original conception was – or is – the true version of constitutionalism. Michel Foucault (inspired by Nietzsche) urged that we make a distinction between the 'origin' (*Ursprung*) and the 'descent' (*Herkunft*) of a concept (Foucault 1996b). We cannot, argued Foucault, fully understand a concept by simply tracing its first occurrence. The historian of ideas – like the genealogist –

must understand the descent of a concept, i.e. how it has evolved in different directions.[9] A concept is, therefore, like a thread. There is no fibre running through the entire thread, only the overlapping of many fibres which *together* constitute the thread. Likewise with constitutionalism. A tradition – like a family – may follow a developmental sequence during which its components will subtly change. Over a long period of time, like in biological evolution, its core may shed or acquire elements, and similarly its morphology may undergo a transformation. The members of the constitutionalist family do not constitute a monolithic bloc, yet like family members they share certain characteristics – they have what Wittgenstein called 'family resemblance' (Wittgenstein 1984: 277). The most important of these characteristics – though not a necessary one – is the doctrine of the 'rule of law', or the *Rechtsstaat*. Again the Jews may serve as an example: neither Saul, David or Solomon had absolute power. Unlike their contemporary colleagues in Babylon or Egypt, the Jewish kings were restricted in their actions by the law as laid down by God. The *Law*, therefore, could not be altered. The Law was literally God-given. The king's role was to apply the law – he was a judge rather than a law-giver – though not all kings adjudicated as wisely as Solomon.

The doctrine of the rule of law might have been invented – or introduced – by the Jews. This people, however, was not the only one to subscribe to the doctrine. Aristotle, an early constitutionalist, advocated a similar doctrine in *The Politics*, noting that the ruler was limited by the natural laws. He believed that 'the law should be sovereign on every issue, and that magistrates and citizens should only decide about details', as the rulers were bound by a higher law (Aristotle 1988–89: 1292a).

Political theorists and practitioners, until Marsilius of Padua, held it undisputed that the law was given by God – or an equivalent figure – and that the ruler could not, and should not, change the law but merely apply it (Vile 1998: 29). The work of Marsilius of Padua in the fourteenth century was a turning point. A little earlier Thomas Aquinas had made a distinction between the ruler's functions of laying down the law and of administering the law (Vile 1998: 30).

Marsilius went much further. By placing the legislative power in the people, and by rejecting the view that positive law must confirm to a higher law, he saw laws as enactments of secular authority. The old doctrine was well-suited to a society which was fundamentally unaltered from the fall of the *Polis* to the Renaissance. The law – as given to Moses, Solon, Romulus – was made for traditional society, and a society that seemed remarkably static. Yet this society, and hence its laws, was becoming an anachronism at the end of the Middle Ages in the Northern Italian city-state cradles of modernity.

Marsilius has, rightly or wrongly, been seen as an early democrat; a champion of populism in an age of clerical despotism. This, however, was not his main contribution. His seminal contribution to the history of political thought was that he instituted man (whether individually or collectively) as the law-giver. The ruler should legislate – not merely adjudicate. The law was not static, God-given; it was to be made by men responding to a changing society. 'The primary and proper efficient cause of the law', wrote Marsilius of Padua in *The Defensor of the Peace* (his main work), 'is the people ... commanding or determining that something should be done or omitted with regard to human civil acts' (Marsilius 1951: 45). The law was no longer static and eternal; it could – and should – be altered when changing social and economic circumstances demanded.

This altered focus opened a Pandora's box in political theory – and did so in a way which nobody had foreseen. For by granting the ruler the right to legislate the inbuilt checks and balances inherent in the classical doctrine were now gone. Not everybody saw this as a problem. The absolutists were in the ascendancy during the Renaissance. Indeed, checks and balances were seen as a hindrance rather than a necessity. Marsilius' doctrine – quite unintentionally – thus paved the way for a re-emergence of despotism as a credible doctrine (a feat that not even the Roman emperors had succeeded in forging). The king – now transformed to *rex dei gratia* – became a lawgiver and a judge anointed by God in the fashionable view. 'Every man that is born', wrote Robert Filmer, 'is so far from being free-born that by subjection he is always to live, unless by immediate appointment from God ... he becomes possessed of that power to which he was subject' (Filmer 1949: 233). A monarch who subscribed to this view was James I, who even troubled himself with penning his political philosophy in the treatise *The Trew Law of Free Monarchs*. James foreshadowed Filmer's theory by noting that 'kings are also compared to fathers of families; for the King is *parens patriae*, the father of his people' (James cited in Fermon 1997: 211).

These works – in themselves philosophically insignificant – owed much to Marsilius, especially as he had been read by Jean Bodin, who in his *Six Livres de la Republique* had argued that a 'well ordered state needs an absolute and legitimate sovereign centre' (McClelland 1996, 281), a doctrine, which – as we have seen – was continued by Thomas Hobbes. Armed with view of Marsilius, Jean Bodin effectively buried the ancient theory of limited government, according to which the king was essentially a judge interpreting an eternal and unchanging law. Bodin asserted that the monarch had the authority to enact new laws to *his* people and – equally importantly (from a historical perspective) – that legislation was the first and chief mark of sovereignty (Vile 1998: 29).

And then it changed. Absolutism gradually lost ground at the end of the seventeenth century. It is difficult to point to one single book or event that challenged the philosophical dominance of absolutism (indeed, absolutism remained the dominant doctrine in practical politics until the American Revolution). Constitutionalism was re-born in England, albeit little by little. The need for independent judges to counter a potentially omnipotent king had been emphasised by George Buchanan as early as 1579 (Vile 1998: 34), and Robert Hooker had asserted in *The Laws of Ecclesiastical Polity* that the king ought not to be judge in cases of felony or treason. Yet it seems difficult to sustain the view that these interventions were but peripheral to the development of constitutionalism. Thus it was not until after the English Civil War that modern constitutionalism took a form which is recognisable today. In the Putney debates[10] Henry Ireton, one of the Levellers, made a case for a system (which he believed had existed before): 'the two great powers of this kingdom are divided betwixt the Lords and the Commons, and it is most probable to me that it was so that it was so that judicial power was in the Lords principally … the legislative power principally in the Commons' (quoted in Vile 1998: 34). This might not have been the first instance of the advocacy of a system of the division of powers but it was indicative of a general trend, and a new tendency to combine the ancient doctrine of constitutionalism with Marsilius' doctrine that man is lawgiver. Algeron Sydney, another of the proto-constitutionalists, writing in 1678 in the aftermath of the English Civil War, stressed the latter:

> It must be acknowledged that the whole fabrick of tyranny will be much weakened if we prove that nations have the right to make their own laws, constitute their own magistrates; and that such as are so constituted owe an account of their actions by whom, and for whom they are appointed. (Sydney 1996: 12)

The same view was more famously developed by John Locke, in his *Second Treatise of Government*. For Locke, the king, while bound by natural law, could only perform his executive power subject to the consent of the people (represented in Parliament). Rejecting Filmer's view, Locke noted that 'he that thinks that absolute power purifies mens' blood, and corrects the baseness of human nature, need read but the history of this, or any other age, to be convinced of the contrary' (Locke 1988: 327). He therefore urged that the 'legislative and the executive' power should be 'separated' (365). Not a new view at this time – indeed, the view had been stated more firmly by the Levellers and Sydney, but a view which only gained acceptance after it had been expressed by Locke.

There is a direct link between this view and the fully fledged doctrine of constitutionalism as the separation of powers, which was developed by Charles Secondat de Montesquieu (who in turn inspired both James Madison and Jean-Jacques Rousseau). In *The Spirit of the Laws* Montesquieu wrote:

> When the legislative and executive powers are united in the same person, or in the same body of magistrates, there can be no liberty … Again, there is no liberty if the judiciary power be not separated from the legislative and executive. Were it joined with the legislative, the life and liberty of the subject would be exposed to arbitrary control; for the judge might behave with violence and oppression. There would be an end to everything, were the same man, or the same body, whether nobles or of the people, to exercise those three powers, that of enacting laws, that of executing the public resolutions, and of trying the cases of individuals. (Montesquieu quoted in Vile 1998: 99)

Thus the history of constitutionalism did not follow a straight path or an orderly evolution. From its haziest origins on Mount Sinai, where rulers for the first time accepted the doctrine that they were bound by a higher law, through Marsilius, to Sydney, Locke and Montesquieu, the doctrine gradually took an institutionalist form, i.e. it was combined with the doctrine of the separation of powers. What remained was to make the doctrine democratic. It was this task that Rousseau sought to resolve.

Rousseau's constitutionalism

Rousseau has traditionally been read as the antithesis of the constitutionalist school. Ernest Barker – to quote but one (one could also mention Hayek, Barry, Talmon and Popper) contends that 'in the last resort Rousseau is a totalitarian' (Barker 1948: xxxviii). The question is whether Rousseau ever held views which deserve to be quoted using these terms? If he, in fact, as often contended, developed a doctrine which was anathema to modern constitutional democracy.

Covering a vast variety of topics, one could be excused for failing to discern a common denominator in Rousseau's thought. Rousseau's *oeuvre politique* deals with issues ranging from constitutional law, through historical sociology and political theory, through comparative government to international politics.[11] Yet all his political works, with the possible exception of *Pologne*, contain two recurrent theses: the necessity of limiting (or placing checks on) executive power, and the impossibility of direct legislation by the people. Rousseau did perhaps become more concerned with practical politics in his later years, yet his views regarding this remained the same.[12]

Direct democracy and checks and balances

Rousseau is often described as an archetypal theorist of direct participation. Carole Pateman, an often-quoted authority on the subject, writes: 'The central function of participation in Rousseau's theory is an educative one, using the term in the widest sense. Rousseau's ideal system is designed to develop responsible, individual social and political action through the effect of the participatory process' (Pateman 1970: 24–5).

Rousseau was, in fact, severely critical of the practice, as well as of the theory, of direct participation (Leigh 1964). In the *Discourse sur l'inégalité* he thus stressed, in direct contradiction of Pateman's thesis: 'In order to prevent self-interested and ill-conceived projects, and all such dangerous innovations as finally ruined the Athenians, each man should not be at liberty to propose new laws at pleasure ... that right should exclusively belong to the magistrates' ('*ce droit appartint aux seuls Magistrats*') (III: 114).

This denunciation of the very system with which he so often – if incorrectly – has been associated (Dicey 1910) was not exceptional. This criticism of direct democracy can be found elsewhere in his political writings. In his *Discourse on Political Economy* he thus rejected that the 'people should be continually assembled to pass laws'. He continued by asking the rhetorical question, 'must the whole nation be assembled together at every unseen event'? His answer was negative. Something which is difficult to translate: '*Faudra-t-il assembler toute la nation à chaque événement imprévû? Il faudra d'autant moins l'assembler.*' He continued noting 'that direct democracy in a great people would be impracticable' ('*Est impracticable dans un grand peuple*') (III: 251).

Historians of political thought are always vulnerable to the charge of quoting out of context. The almost inherently contradictory nature of Rousseau's writings seems to justify a whole array of readings (Wokler 1995: 119). However, it is noteworthy that he consistently and without exception stressed his opposition to direct legislation by the people. *Du Contrat Social*, arguably his *chef d'oeuvre*, is no exception. Consistent with the view in his earlier writings he contended that, 'one can hardly imagine that all the people would sit permanently in an assembly to deal with public affairs' ('*on ne peut imaginer que le peuple reste inccassament assemblé pour vaquer aux affairees publique*') (III: 404).

These quotes do not paint a picture of an anti-democrat, they rather amount to an almost Burkean theory of representation. While there are remarkable and perhaps surprising similarities between Burke and Rousseau (as we have already argued above),[13] it would be erroneous to cite him as an opponent of all forms of citizen participation, let alone as being opposed to democracy – as we use the term today. Rousseau agreed with Montesquieu (see Book XI.6 of *Spirit of the Laws*), and later with Burke (Burke 1902: 447), that representative government was necessary. But he would not have been in agreement with the Burke that the representatives should act at their own discretion, as this would leave the people vulnerable to encroachments by the former.

Rousseau did write, in a letter to d'Ivernois, 'it is evident that I am not a visionary, and that, in *Du Contrat Social*, I did not defend democracy' (quoted in Wokler 1995: 111), yet Rousseau, like political theorists from Aristotle through Spinoza to Madison, uses the term democracy to refer to pure and direct democratic participation (like in Athens),[14] a system which Rousseau had deemed unrealistic and undesirable.

Rousseau favoured an 'aristocratic system', in which the representatives should propose the laws. This system was, as Masters has noted, 'merely another name for parliamentary or representative government' (Masters 1968: 402).[15] Rousseau writes: 'There are three types of aristocracy; natural, elective and hereditary. The first is suited only to primitive people, the third is the worst of all governments, the second is the best, and this is aristocracy in the true sense of the word' (III: 406). Rousseau agreed with Montesquieu that the 'great advantage of representatives is their capacity for discussing politics', an activity for which the 'people collectively are extremely unfit' (Montesquieu 1989, XI: 6). Yet he did not agree with Montesquieu that public participation was 'a great fault', and that 'they [the people] ought to have no share in government but for the choosing of representatives'. Leaving legislation to the discretion of the representatives would leave the people vulnerable to the encroachments of power by their elected masters. It was this lack of a check on the representatives, and the accompanying risks that they, the representatives, could vote contrary to the *General Will*, that made checks necessary. Burke had famously told the electors in Bristol that 'your representative owes you not your industry alone but his judgement and he betrays instead of serving you if he sacrifices it to your opinion' (Burke 1902, 447). This problem would not, in Rousseau's opinion, be resolved through representative government alone, but by complementing it with referendums in which the people could hold the magistrates accountable for their decisions. 'The holders of executive office are not the people's masters but its officer', and, wrote Rousseau, 'the people can appoint them and dismiss them as it pleases' (*'qu'il peut les établir et les destituer quand il lui plait'*) (III: 434).

Like *The Federalist*, Rousseau wanted these aristocrats to be elected by the people. He outlines this theory in *Du Contrat Social*: '[under direct democracy] all the citizens are born magistrates, while this other system [elected aristocracy] limits itself to a small number of magistrates, every one of whom is elected, a method which makes honesty, sagacity, experience and all the other grounds of popular preference and esteem further guarantees of wise government' (III: 407). Similarly in the *Project de la Corse*; 'what Corsica needs is a mixed government ['*Gouvernement mixte*'], where the people assemble by sections rather than by whole, and where the repositories of its power are changed at frequent intervals' (III: 907). In all his political writings he stressed that the power of any political institution should be kept in check. A view, which in turn, resulted in the development of a theory, which in some respects resembled modern models of social choice (Trachtenberg 1993). Rousseau's interest in policy failures is evidently based on the epistemological view, which stresses the fallibility of human knowledge and, consequently, the most unplatonic view that no one has privileged access to the general will. Contrary to the charge that Rousseau's political philosophy would lead to authoritarianism (as the rulers would claim to be the only ones who fathomed *la volonté général*, whereas the ordinary citizen should be 'forced to be free' (*'qu'en le forcera d'être libre'*) (III: 364) by the benevolent, if autocratic, rulers), he explicitly stressed this danger. Rousseau emphasised that '*tout homme peut graver du Pierre ou achté un oracle*', 'any man can carve tablets of stone, or bribe an oracle, train a bird to whisper in his ear, or discover some vulgar means of imposing himself on the people' (III: 384). Rousseau, in other words, anticipated the likes of Stalin, Robespierre and Pol Pot, indeed, it was the aim of his political philosophy to rid society from tyrants. Alas not all of his followers and interpreters have understood this.

Rousseau's concept of *la volonté général* was not, therefore, a mystic concept of abstract political theology. It was rather theoretically related to the concept of 'collective goods', as employed by rational choice theorists (Mueller 1996: 51). Using this framework, one can see the identification and implementation of the General Will as a social welfare problem, and 'some of the most obscure passages can be clarified' (Grofman and Feld 1988: 567). Through this approach we might resolve the often misunderstood assertion in Du Contrat Social that the *Will of All* is not – necessarily – the *General Will*. Far from basing this view on metaphysics, Rousseau, arguably, hinted at an early variant of Arrow's theorem, namely that it is impossible – or at least very difficult – to aggregate the individual preferences to a social welfare function (Trachtenberg 1993: 52). That is, Rousseau, criticised the will of all on the ground that it 'cannot serve as a reliable basis of social co-operation; he presumes that people will not co-operate to provide the collective welfare' (Trachtenberg 1993: 14).[16]

While it would be anachronistic to attach twentieth-century labels to an eighteenth-century theorist, it is noteworthy how preoccupied Rousseau was with the inherent difficulties of aggregating preferences and resolving *collective action problems*, something which, perhaps, is most visible in the fable of the stag hunt in the *Discourse on Inequality*. He wrote:

> men were able imperceptibly to acquire some crude idea of mutual commitments and the advantage of fulfilling them, but only as far as present and palpable interest could demand, for foresight meant nothing to them, and far from being interested in a distant future, they hardly thought of the next day. If it was a matter of catching a deer, each certainly felt strongly that for this purpose he ought to remain on his post, but if a hare happened to pass within reach of one of them, it must not be doubted that he pursued it without scruple, and that having caught his prey, troubled himself very little about having caused his companions to miss theirs. (III: 167)

While each individual realised the benefits of co-operation, he was reluctant to give up modest short-term benefits for greater long-term gains. The establishment of co-operation was not, therefore, a foregone conclusion, although Rousseau believed that individuals in the fullness of time had learned to appreciate – at least some of – the benefits of collective action (Grofman and Feld 1988: 537).

It was the realisation that co-operation was necessary that led to the establishment of *le contrat social* (exactly as in Hobbes' *De Cive*).[17] As Rousseau put it in *The Geneva Manuscript*;

> If the clashing of particular interests make the establishment of civil societies necessary, the agreement of these very interests make it possible. The common element in these different interests is what forms the social tie; and were there no point of agreement between them, no society would exist. (III: 282)

Yet the question remained

> How to find a form of association, which will defend the persons and goods
> of each member with the collective force of all, and under which each
> individual, while uniting himself with others, obeys no one but himself,
> and remains as free as before? (III: 360)

True to his republican inclinations Rousseau found the answer in a system
under which, 'each one of us puts into the community his person and all
his powers under the supreme direction of the General Will' (III: 360). Yet
he admitted – which often has gone unnoticed – that this system was far
from flawless. As nobody had privileged access to the General Will it was
important that power be shared lest a group of representatives usurped
that power which rightfully belonged to the citizens. The citizens had to
keep the magistrates in check. Sovereignty could only be represented by
all citizens (the representatives are merely the people's 'agents and cannot
decide anything finally').

The 'English people' were therefore 'unfree' (III: 429) because once they
have delegated power they could not – and cannot – control the
government, or the 'elected dictatorship', to use the late Lord Hailsham's
apt phrase. Rousseau did not, therefore, want to abolish representative
government, but merely to complement this system with mechanisms of
direct participation of the citizens, lest the delegates should transgress the
boundaries of their authority. His swipe against the English was not a
total dismissal of the British constitution. Indeed, he praised the
Westminster system in *Lettres écrites de la montagne* (III: 848). What he
merely wanted to show was that Britain – at that time the only major
power to hold elections – was not an ideal polity.

In developing a model of constitutionalism, Rousseau stressed that the
people should be entitled to veto legislation lest the enactments of the
representatives should be in contravention of the General Will, i.e. represent
the *Particular* as opposed to the *General Will*. It was in order to prevent
this encroachment that he concluded that any law 'which has not been
ratified by the people in person is void, is not a law at all' (III: 430).

This preoccupation with the danger that the political system might be
corrupted – through unlimited rule – is in stark contrast to the reception
– or *Wirkungsgeschichte* – of Rousseau's work, especially in the English-
speaking world (see Cobban 1968 for an overview). The thinker whom
Karl Popper denounced as a champion of unchecked rule of the majority
(Popper 1945: 50) did, in fact, advocate a system of (a variant of) balances
of power. Not surprising, perhaps, as historians have documented his

indebtedness to Montesquieu (Cranston 1986: 16). This support for a system of checks and balances is nowhere more evident than in *Lettres écrites de la Montagne*. Rousseau asks rhetorically: 'What better government is there than one of which all parts are held in perfect equilibrium, where the individuals cannot transgress the law because they are subject to magistrates, and the magistrates cannot transgress it because they are supervised by the people?' (III: 844).

Rousseau's originality lay not least in his proposed solution to what James Madison, in *Federalist Paper 63*, called 'the continual encroachment' of the rulers (Hamilton 1961: 389). While most constitutionalists have sought to resolve the problem through elitist means – the exception is Dicey (1910) – for example through constitutional courts (Hamilton), bi-cameralism (Montesquieu), consociational powersharing (Althusius) – Rousseau proposed (like the American populists a century later)[18] that the most effective and legitimate check on power was the plebiscite – or referendum as it has become generally known. As already alluded to, Rousseau proposed a system under which the citizens should perform the function of a 'people's second chamber' by consenting, or otherwise, to acts passed by the representative assembly. True to his reverence for the Romans (whose system of government he elsewhere describes as, 'the best government that have ever existed' (*la police plus favourable à la constitution de l'Etat*) (III, 809) he cites (a somewhat idealised) description of the Roman Republic 200 BC in support of his views:[19] 'the decemvirs themselves never claimed the right to pass any laws merely on their own authority. Nothing we propose to you, they said to the people, can pass into law without your consent' (*ne peut passer en loi sans votre con-sentement*) (III, 382).[20] This was a revolutionary proposal at the time – and indeed it remains to be. True Locke had, in *Second Treatise*, argued that 'if a controversie arise betwixt a Prince and some of the People, in a matter where the law is silent, or doubtful, and the thing be of great Consequence, I think that the proper Umpire in such a case should be the body of the People' (Locke 1988, 427). Yet the Englishman had not explained or outlined how matters were to be resolved in the people's favour. Rousseau did. The people were to decide through direct voting. He was not the last one to reach this conclusion. One hundred and fifty years later A.V. Dicey – a noted British constitutionalist – reached the same conclusion (and one which, like Rousseau's, showed the shortcomings of Madison's system). Dicey explained:

> The referendum has one pre-eminent recommendation, not possessed by any of the artful, or ingenious, devices for strengthening the power of the

second chamber, or placing a veto in the hands of a minority. Its application does not cause irritation. If the Lords[the second chamber in the British system] reject a Bill people demand the reform of the peerage; if the French Senate (a popularly elected body) hesitates to approve a revision of the Constitution, the next scheme for revision contains a clause for the abolition of the Senate. Popular pride is roused, voters are asked to make it a point of honour that a measure, which an aristocratic or select chamber has rejected, shall be carried. A Bill's rejection turns into a reason for its passing into law. Should a regular appeal to the electors result in the rejection of a Bill passed by Parliament, this childish irritation becomes an impossibility. The people cannot be angered at the act of the people. (Dicey quoted in Qvortrup 2002: 65)

Rousseau held the same view. While defending the necessity of representative government, he was adamant that the representative body should not usurp the functions of the people.[21] While admitting the theoretical benefits of the absolutist doctrine of undivided rule, Rousseau reiterated his preference for a division of powers:

He who makes the laws knows better than anyone how it should be executed and interpreted. So it might seem that there could be no better constitution than one, which united the executive power with the legislative; in fact this very union makes that form of government deficient (*qui rend ce gouvernement insuffisant*). It is not good that he who makes the laws should execute it. (III: 404)

Rousseau explicitly favoured checks and balances: 'the legislative power consists of two things inseparably linked: to make laws and to maintain them, that is to say, to supervise the executive power … without it [the power of supervision] there is no relation, no subordination between the two powers, the one would depend on the other' (III: 837). Or, as he put it in *Du Contrat Social*; 'the man who frames the laws has not, or ought not to have any legislative rights' ('*celui qui rédige les lois n'a donc ou ne droit avoir aucun droit législatif*') (III: 383).

Is the plebiscite a safeguard?

However, one might question if these plebiscitary devices would prevent the corruption of power. Citing the undemocratic use of plebiscites by Napoleon III, Melvin Richter has criticised Rousseau for paving the way towards a 'plebiscitary dictatorship' (Richter 1995: 71), as a rigged referendum, in reality, may legitimise a publicly sanctioned autocracy. This view was forcefully summed up by Michael Oakeshott: 'The plebiscite is not a method by which 'mass man' imposes his choice upon his rulers; it is a method for generating a government with unlimited authority to make choices on his behalf. In the plebiscite 'mass man' achieved final release from the burden of individuality: he was emphatically told what to choose' (Oakeshott 1991: 379).

There are certainly an abundance of plebiscites which have generated dictators with unlimited powers, e.g. the plebiscites sponsored by Hitler. Rousseau himself was not blind to the danger that demagogues could deceive the people; 'the people', he wrote, 'is never corrupted, it is often misled, and only then does it want what is bad' (III: 371). Empirical evidence does not support this scepticism, however; Charles de Gaulle lost the plebiscite on local government in 1969 and even General Pinochet was forced to step down when 56 per cent of the voters rejected a proposal which would have extended his powers. Whether referendums result in 'plebiscitary dictatorship' is ultimately an empirical question, but evidence does not readily support this thesis. This conclusion does not imply that Rousseau's model was realistic – let alone meant to be. Rousseau was a theorist not a politician. We can be inspired by the classics; they do speak through the ages but they have not provided us with solutions, let alone with applicable schemes for reform. Whether realistic or not, Rousseau's considerations on a system of representative government, kept in check by a scheme of plebiscitary checks and balances, provides food for thought for constitutional engineers and political theorists alike.

Constitutionalism and beyond?

Rousseau was – albeit among other things – a constitutionalist and a republican who combined two opposite poles of democratic theory. As did formal minimalists, like Madison and Montesquieu, he made a case for representative government, and, like participationists, he encouraged more direct and robust modes of popular engagement in politics. By combining these two approaches, Rousseau not only developed an alternative check on the power of the elites, he also – and equally importantly – combined their respective strengths and weaknesses. Minimalists rightly stress the necessity of deliberation, and point out that this is only possible under indirect democracy. However, they overlook the flip-side of representative government, such as log-rolling and rent-seeking (Qvortrup 2002: 153). Participationists – like, say, Benjamin Barber – rightly stress the edifying aspects of civic engagement, yet tend to overlook the danger of populism, as well as they underestimate the practical difficulties in institutionalising direct legislation. Politics is not a spectator sport.

Through his case for referendums, Rousseau was able to both ensure the elements of deliberation, as well as introducing a democratically legitimate check on the elites. It is through this theory that Rousseau succeeds in drawing a line between direct and representative democracy and to combine the best of both systems. This is an important contribution, not only to political theory, but also for practical politicians who advocate the greater use of referendums as a complement to representative government, yet stop short of endorsing law-making by the people.

This essay does not aspire to be the last word on Rousseau's constitutional doctrine. The works of the classics are never mono-dimensional, but always open to interpretation. Rousseau was assuredly *not* a liberal constitutionalist like, say, Mill, yet his 'theory' of constitutionalism was a good deal closer to other constitutionalist theories than is commonly assumed. Far from presenting a theory of political theology about the *General Will*, he developed a model which, in fact, can be seen as a precursor of modern-day political science.

'My defence for the people's right to veto legislation passed by the representatives', wrote Dicey, was 'not due to any increased enthusiasm for the principles preached by Rousseau' (Dicey 1910: 539). It is conspicuous that Dicey singled out Rousseau as the straw man of direct democracy run amok. In reality Dicey – through developing a doctrine of people's vetoes – advocated the very same system as had been developed by Rousseau. Yet, while Dicey has been canonised by constitutionalists, such as Hayek (1960: 240), Rousseau has been vilified by the very same scholars. There may be several self-inflicted reasons for this, including Rousseau's poetic style, yet the substance of his writings indicates that constitutionalists should embrace rather than reject him, though Rousseau, in fairness, is not the average constitutionalist.

Censorship and the education of democratic man

The reader might be excused for thinking that Rousseau – as he was presented above – was but a liberal constitutionalist with a bit of a twist. Such a conclusion would not be an original one (it was the thrust of John W. Chapman's study (Chapman, 1968),[22] nor, more importantly, would this be an entirely valid conclusion. Proponents of the constitutionalist interpretation, the present author included (Qvortrup 2002), find it difficult to square his democratic and constitutionalist views with his seemingly contradictory, but unequivocal, arguments for censorship. In *Du Contrat Social* Rousseau noted that 'men always love what is good or what they *think* is good, but it is in their judgement that they err; hence it is their judgement that has to be regulated' (III: 459). Such views are provocative and repulsive at a time when Mill's attack on censorship in *On Liberty* received justified support. The English liberal noted that 'the opinion which it is attempted to suppress by authority may possibly be true. Those who desire to suppress it, of course, deny its truth but they are not infallible … All silencing of discussion is an assumption of infallibility' (Mill 1861: 22).[23] This presumed infallibility is difficult to square with Rousseau's scepticism in general and his political views in particular. Such is the power of Mill's view (and creeds like it) that we often forget that the republicans began 'from the presupposition that a free society governed by its members is in need of the most careful education in order that the citizens have the requisite virtues for ruling themselves and one another' (Bloom 1996: xi). Republican freedom, the granting to a people the right to legislate for themselves, is a grave task, which requires a concerted effort, and one which not only required a scheme of negative education but also – and more controversially (for us at least) – an element of censorship. 'Freedom', Rousseau wrote in *Considérations sur la gouvernement du Pologne*, 'is a food that is good to taste but hard to digest: it settles well only on a good strong stomach' (III: 974). It may seem strange today that the monarchical government was more tolerant than the republican city-state. In those days, it was quite common that republics required the greatest self-imposed restraints whereas tyrannies and other decadent regimes could often afford the greatest individual liberties. Indeed, Goethe (one of Rousseau's most illustrious – and independent-minded – disciples) observed in *Faust*, that 'he who does not daily conquer freedom deserves it not' ('*nur der verdient sich Freiheit wie das Leben, der täglich sie erobern muss*') (Goethe 2001: 203) would have received Rousseau's whole hearted support. Yet while Rousseau was – in theory – fond of censorship he was sceptical as regards the practicality of implementing such a scheme. And while he talked about reaching 'deep into men's hearts and uproot it by implanting healthier and more noble tastes', he conceded that 'merely prohibiting the things … is a clumsy expedient and a pointless one, unless you see to it first that those things are hated and despised' (V: 18).

The problem with the liberal perspective is that it assumes that an atomistic society is possible; that it is possible to have rights without duties. Modern man, Rousseau noted in his *Letter to M. D'Alembert on the Theatre*, resembles the man

> who did not want to get out of bed although the house was on fire. 'The house is burning', they yelled at him. 'What difference does that make to

me?' he answered. 'I am only renting it.' Finally, the fire reached him. Immediately, he bounded out, ran, screamed, and became disturbed. He began to understand that sometimes we must take an interest in the house we live in even though it does not belong to us. (Rousseau 1960: 42)

This is a portrait of the *bourgeois*, that is of a man who, 'in dealing with others think only of himself, and … in dealing with himself thinks only of others' (Bloom cited in Froese 2002: 34). Yet a society of egoists is an impossibility. The bourgeois is a parasite who abuses the sacrifices of others – i.e. more civic-minded citizens. If all people pursued their own goals the result would be the breakdown of society, hence the necessity of political education – and even censorship. Not, it must be stressed, as a means of indoctrinating the citizens but rather as a mechanism for generating an understanding of social cohesion, and an appreciation of the fundamental maxim that there can be no rights without duties. Citizenship has to be taught. We must learn to strive for things that are greater than self-glory or personal gratification. The citizen must be given a sense that citizenship – in return for political and social rights – must serve the state, and that he, if need be, must sacrifice *himself* for the sake of the common good. This, needless to say, was easier said than done. Rousseau did not – unlike Aristotle[24] – consider man as a social animal but as an individualist; a virtuous anarchist. He consistently stressed how difficult it was for us to learn to be – and perceive ourselves as – a part of a corporate whole to which we belong and from which we draw so much of our sustenance. In *The Social Contract* he described the task as 'so to speak, changing human nature', or 'denaturing' us (III: 381). Censorship was necessary to prevent man from acquiring views which would undermine his civic responsibilities. It was not, however, intended to shape man in a totalitarian mould; 'the censorial office', he admits, 'may be useful in preserving morals, but never in restoring them' (III: 479). The censorial office role would probably be no other than it is in most modern countries today, i.e. where there are restrictions on children and young people's access to violent and pornographic films and videos. What was important was that citizens needed to be guided in the direction of civic duties to fulfil obligations. Allan Bloom – that most perceptive observer of Rousseau – has commented that we have to 'distinguish between the really important elements of our liberty and the pretenders, which have gained credit by assimilating themselves to the truly necessary and noble pursuits; the fate of the most cherished rights should not be bound up with that of a licence and self-indulgence incapable of resisting impartial examination' (Bloom 1960: xiii). Censorship may be necessary to ensure that we keep on the path of righteousness.

Rousseau did not believe that these mechanisms would rid society of its ills once and for all. He was not a utopian. Politics would not become automatic; the good society required good citizens. 'The greatest public authority', he wrote, 'lies in the hearts of its citizens ... nothing can take the place of morality in government. It is not only upright men who know how to administer the laws but *at bottom only good men who know how to obey them*' (III: 252, italics added). In short, man should learn to become a good and virtuous citizen. Not an easy task but one we all must learn.

His ambition was to create a virtuous circle in which transformed human beings could live in a transformed society in which all could equally enjoy a sense of self-fulfilment and community with others. This could not be established in a society dominated by competitive self-interested behaviour, which he believed had created inequality and social exploitation. Establishing morals – engendering a sense of community and solidarity with our fellow citizens – may require primary education, but this education has subsequently to be followed up by civic activities. There are thus two strands to Rousseau's education of democratic man; the education of the child (see below) and the continuing civic education of the citizen once he has come of age.

Rousseau, believing that 'Everything is good that leaves the hands of the creator of all things' (IV: 279), maintained that the first task of the educationalist was to rediscover original man. His proposed education was a negative one, one of a discovery of the original man. He sought – in the eminent words of Jean Starobinsky – to rediscover 'a forgotten present, a form that remained intact behind the veils' (Starobinsky 1988, 19). The aim of this 'negative education' was to re-find *compassion* and *amour de soi même*, those natural feelings which have given way to vanity, selfishness, *amour propre*. Only once this had been accomplished could man begin his apprenticeship as a citizen. We find the most eloquent expression of this in *La Nouvelle Heloïse*. In a discussion with Saint-Preux and Wolmar, Julie claims that *pitié* is a natural feeling, and that the aim of education is to appeal to this natural goodness – not to create some inauthentic sense of abstract duties. 'As far as I am concerned', says Julie, 'I am seeking to stay clear of the idea of what one ought to or should do, I never give him [her child] reason to believe that you should serve others out of pure duty; rather he should [serve others] out of compassion. This is, perhaps, the most important and difficult part of education' (II: 564).

A society can only survive if its citizens have compassion with their fellow citizens and if they realise the necessity of partaking in civic functions with the aim of self-preservation. Liberals (the heirs of Smith and Locke) seem to be labouring under the delusion that society is somehow automatic, that man is entitled to act without any external constraints and that as this egotistical pursuit of personal happiness, moreover, is believed to result in the greatest happiness of all, it is a justification for this course of action. Rousseau, whilst supporting checks on executive power and the state, rejected this as fanciful. Republican virtues do not emerge in a vacuum; 'citizens cannot be formed in a day, and in order to have them as men it is necessary to educate them as children' (III: 259–60). Society can only be maintained if man is willing and able to trade in his limitless 'negative' freedom for the benefit of the whole of the community. Or, as he writes elsewhere, in language which is bound to be misunderstood, 'Good social institutions are those that best know how to denature man, to take his absolute existence from him in order to give him a relative one and transport him into the common unity, with the result that each individual believes himself no longer one but a part of the unity and no longer feels except within the whole' (Rousseau 1979a: 250).

Rousseau might have exaggerated when he noted that 'every amusement is an evil for a being whose life is so short and whose time is so precious' (Rousseau 1960: 16). Yet his observation that failure to engage in active citizenship, which in turn has to be fostered, is indisputable. The aim of all institutions is to 'strengthen the national character, to augment the natural inclinations, and to give energy to all the passions' (20). That this required political education is a truism which liberals conveniently tend to overlook. Rousseau was not a liberal. And while he was a constitutionalist, he was more than that. Man needs to be continually re-taught that organic solidarity is a necessary condition for social cohesion. God made man capable of goodness, as Rousseau noted in the introduction to *Emile*, alas man, when left to his own devices, did not earn the trust of his heavenly Father. Hence it was necessary for God in his grace to send his son to remind man that he was created in God's image, and to teach man that he was capable of goodness, if only he could strip himself of ungodly humanism and *amour propre*. Man, therefore, is endowed with goodness, not with original sin (as postulated by Augustin). As Rousseau lets Saint Preux utter:

> In creating man he [God] endowed him with all the faculties needed for his accomplishment of what was required of him, and when we ask him for the power to do good, we ask him for nothing he has not already given us. He has given us reason to discern what is good, conscience to love it, and freedom to choose it. It is in these sublime gifts that divine grace consists, and since

we have received them, we are all accountable for them. (quoted in Riley 2001: 108)

For Rousseau, therefore, the resolution to the problem of human morals did not lie in establishing institutions which would utilise man's selfishness for the benefit of mankind. Like Tocqueville, Rousseau saw societies essentially regulated by 'the feelings, the beliefs, the ideas, the habits of the heart and mind that compose them' (Rousseau cited in Riley 2001: 35), not just by institutions. 'There will never be a good and solid constitution unless the law rules over the hearts of the citizens', he wrote in the *Government of Poland* (35). The problem with man, as conceived by Hobbesians (and later by utilitarians like Bentham and modern economists) was that they, in their concern for their own wellbeing, had failed to recognise that society, to paraphrase Christ, 'does not live off bread alone'. In his pursuit of his own happiness man forgets his responsibilities to society, and that he is responsible for maintaining social order. Sacrifice for the common good was the model in Rome. However, being a realist, Rousseau conceded that a Roman solution was no longer possible, as public instruction 'no longer exists, because where there is no longer a fatherland, there can no longer be citizens' (35). In other writings – namely in *Considérations sur la gouvernement du Polonge*, *The Constitution of Corsica* and partly in *Du Contrat Social*, he sought to re-establish and re-develop the ancient concept of patriotism into the modern doctrine of nationalism. This doctrine is the subject of the next chapter.

Notes

1 The classic contribution to this literature is Hannah Arendt, *The Origins of Totalitarianism* (New York: Meridian, 1958).

2 Jean Fabre (1962), 'Realité et Utopie dans la Pensée de Rousseau, in *Annales de Societé Jean-Jacques Rousseau*, Tome 45, 1959–62.

3 R.A. Leigh noted: 'even if we accept this seemingly impossible challenge, it is clear that so far as it concerns Rousseau's intentions there is not much need to argue' (Leigh, *Rousseau et son Oeuvre* (Paris: Klinckseik, 1964).

4 This distinction can also be found in Robert Derathé, *Jean-Jacques Rousseau et la science politique de son temps* (Paris: J. Vrin, 1988), p. 365.

5 'A multitude of men are made one person, when they are by one man or one person represented.' (Thomas Hobbes, *Leviathan*, London: Everyman 1973), p. 107.

6 Rousseau only refers only once to Descartes in *Du Contrat Social* (III: 388). There are only two other references to Descartes in his other political writings,

namely in *The Origin of Inequality* (III: 114) and in the *Geneva Manuscript* (III: 321). There are, by contrast, more than sixty references to Hobbes and more than thirty references to Machiavelli.

7 Rousseau was not, of course, an epistemologist. His mildly sceptical position might be summed up in a letter to Deschamps. He writes 'I would love metaphysical truth just as much if I believed it could be found, but I have never found it … I have beliefs, not certain knowledge' (L. 1437).

8 See K. Popper, *Unended Quest* (London: Routledge, 1992). See also Locke's distinction between *real essence* and *nominal essence*.

9 This idea that the history of political concepts is like a family tree is found not only in Foucault. A similar understanding – though a more radical (and nominalistic one) – can be found in the later Wittgenstein, especially in *Philosophical Investigations*. 'Wittgenstein asks us to consider … the proceedings we call "games". What is the essence or the core of the word game? What property or characteristic is common to all things we call games? I mean board-games, ball games, Olympic games, and so on. Don't say; "there *must* be something common, or they would not be called games" – but look and see whether there is anything common to them' John W. Darford, *Wittgenstein and Political Philosophy. A Re-examination of the Foundations of Social Science* (Chicago: University of Chicago, 1978), p. 97. See also Ludwig Wittgenstein, *Philosophische Untersuchungen*, in Wittgenstein, *Gesamtausgabe* (Frankfurt am Main: Suhrkamp, 1984), vol. 1, p. 66.

10 The Putney debates were held in Putney (near London) by the Council of Oliver Cromwell's New Model Army and attended by two officers and two agitators from each regiment . They revealed deep divergence between the two groups, with Cromwell and Ireton resisting the radical demands of the ranks, among whom there was strong support for the Levellers. The Levellers' position has often – through erroneously – been seen as the first example of a demand for universal suffrage. Yet, as C.B. MacPherson has shown, 'the Levellers consistently excluded from their franchise two substantial categories of men, namely servants and wage-earners'. C.B. Macpherson, *The Political Theory of Possessive Individualism. Hobbes to Locke* (Oxford, Oxford University Press, 1962), p. 107.

11 See especially Jean Starobinsky, 'The Political Thought of Jean-Jacques Rousseau', in A. Ritter and J. Bondanella (eds) *Rousseau's Political* Writings (New York: W.W. Norton, 1988), p. 221.

12 Spink, among others, sees *Lettres écrites de la montagne* as the first of three – the others are *Pologne* and *Projet du Corse* – practical works. Instead of 'setting aside the facts', as he puts it in *Discours sur l'inégalité* (III: 132), he now argues on the basis of facts. The theorist Rousseau gradually became the empiricist Rousseau, but he remained a believer in representative democracy – tempered by direct participation and the veto power of the citizens. Spink cited in R. Fralin, *Rousseau and Representation: A Study of the Development of his Concept of Political Institutions* (New York: Columbia University Press, 1978), p. 96.

13 However, David Cameron notes 'When the names Jean-Jacques Rousseau and Edmund Burke are mentioned together, it is usually to illustrate opposite extremes of opinion' (Cameron, *The Social Thought of Rousseau and Burke* (London: Weidenfeld and Nicholson, 1973), p. 1).

14 See, for example, James Madison, 'The Federalist X'. By democracy he meant 'a society consisting of a small number of citizens who assemble and administer laws in person'. Madison 'Federalist X', in Publius, *The Federalist Papers* (New York: Mentor, 1961), p. 81. ('Publius' was the pseudonym under which Madison wrote.)

15 A similar conclusion has been reached by Robert Derathé, who contends that Rousseau gradually came to accept representative government, not simply out of expediency, but as a matter of principle (Derathé, *Jean-Jacques Rousseau et la science politique de son temps* (Paris: J. Vrin, 1988), p. 388).

16 It is, perhaps, instructive to compare this view with John Charvet's conclusion that 'Rousseau's intellectual effort in educational, moral and political theory is conceived as a solution to the problem that arises when natural men become aware of each other and begin to impinge on and conflict with each other' (Charvet 1974, 145).

17 Hobbes writes: 'Those who met together with the intention to erect a city were, almost in the very act of meeting, a democracy.' Hobbes, *Leviathan*, p. 197.

18 See especially Thomas Cronin, *Direct Democracy* (Cambridge: Harvard University Press, 1989), pp. 43–5.

19 Plebiscites were introduced rather late, namely in 287 BC (J.P. McCormick, 'Machiavellian Democracy: Controlling Elites with Ferocious Populism', *American Political Science Review*, vol. 95 (2001), 304). See also L. Taylor, *Roman Voting Assemblies* (Ann-Arbor: University of Michigan Press, 1990).

20 The Roman system was, apparently, inspired by the Athenian democracy. The Decemvirs were, according to Levy, established to increase public participation. The people, he argues, wanted a system of laws 'which every individual citizen could feel he had not only consented to accept but had actually himself proposed' (J. Levy, *The Early History of Rome* (New York: Penguin, 1971), p. 221). It was the latter aspect – the de facto use of legislative initiatives – to which Rousseau referred when he noted that, while advocating the citizens' involvement, he 'would not have liked plebiscites' (III: 113).

21 The same conclusion was reached by American president Teddy Roosevelt. He argued: 'I believe in the referendum, which should not be used to destroy representative government, but to correct it whenever it becomes misrepresentative' (Roosevelt quoted in M. Qvortrup, *A Comparative Study of Referendums. Government by the People* (Manchester: Manchester University Press, 2002), p. 152.

22 See also Lester G. Crocker, *Rousseau's Social Contract: An Interpretative Essay* (Cleveland, Case Western Reserve Press, 1968)), Tanguy L'Aminot (ed.), *Politique et Révolution chez Jean-Jacques Rousseau* (Oxford: Voltaire

Foundation, 1994); Robert Thiéry (ed.), *Rousseau, l''Emile', et la Révolution* (Paris: Universitas, 1992).

23 J.S. Mill, it will be remembered, was anything but liberal. In Chapter VIII of *Considerations on Representative Government* he thus advocated that graduates should be given two votes to prevent the uneducated from gaining influence. Interestingly – and rather incredibly – this system existed in Britain until the late 1940s. See Robert Blackburn, *The Electoral System in the United Kingdom* (London: Macmillan, 1996).

24 In *The Politics*, Aristotle – in classical teleological fashion – noted 'if earlier forms of society are natural so is the state, for it is the end for them [men], and the natural for a thing is its end. For what each is when fully developed, we call its nature, whether we are speaking of a man, a horse, or a family ... Hence it is evident that the state is the creation of nature' (Aristotle, *The Politics* (Cambridge: Cambridge University Press, 1984), p. 3.

4

A civic profession of faith: Rousseau's and nationalism

When Heinrich Heine, the German poet, visited Italy in 1828 he noted in his diary:

> It is as if World History is seeking to become spiritual ... she has a great task. What it is? It is emancipation. Not just the emancipation of the Irish, the Greeks, the Jews and the Blacks of the West Indies. No, the emancipation of the whole world, especially in Europe, where the peoples have reached maturity. (Heine quoted in Gell 1998: 13)

In seeking national self-determination Heine was preaching a new doctrine, one which had been unknown a couple of centuries before. Elie Kedouri observed – perhaps not entirely accurately – that 'Nationalism is a political doctrine invented in Europe at the beginning of the Nineteenth Century' (Kedouri 1960: 1). This might have been an exaggeration but Kedouri had a point. Nationalism is not only regarded as a relatively recently established ideology, it is also regarded as a fatherless doctrine, without the illustrious intellectual ancestry which characterises socialism, liberalism, and even conservatism. Nationalism, it is asserted, lacks a coherent philosophical basis and does not have an intellectual founding father. In Benedict Anderson's words: 'unlike most other isms, nationalism has never produced its great thinkers; no Hobbeses, Tocquevilles, Marxes or Webers' (Anderson 1981: 5).[1] This view seemingly ignores the theory of nationalism developed by Rousseau before the nineteenth century.[2] Rousseau is rarely given full credit for his contribution to the development of the doctrine of nationalism. Unmentioned by Gellner (1983; 1996) and Miller (1995), Rousseau is only mentioned in passing by Anderson (1983) and Hobsbawm (1991). Kedouri acknowledges that Rousseau's *Considérations sur la gouvernement du polonge* (Rousseau 1771 [1985]) influenced nationalist theoreticians (most notably Fichte), yet he maintains that 'Rousseau [did] not provide a complete and rounded theory of the state, a theory which embraces first and last things, and which can proceed only from a unified and systematic vision of the universe' (Kedouri 1960: 33). Further, Rousseau's status as a theoretician of nationalism is overlooked even by Rousseau scholars.[3] Nationalism does not feature in the authoritative works on Rousseau's political philosophy. Rousseau's writings on nationalism are mainly contained in two treatises (although traces can be found elsewhere); in *Projet de Constitution pour la Corse* (1764) and in *Considérations sur la gouvernement du Pologne* (1771). In *Du Contrat Social* Rousseau availed himself for advice on constitutional engineering to nations that were entitled 'to be taught by some wise man how to preserve freedom' (III: 391). Two countries requested his services: Corsica in 1764 and Poland in 1770.

In 1764 he was invited by Mathieu Buttafuoco (a former French soldier and Corsican nobleman) to draw up a constitution for Corsica. This request came against the backdrop of considerable tensions and civil war on the island. In 1735 the Corsicans had revolted against their masters, Genoa. Although Genoese rule was restored in 1748, the revolt resumed in 1752 under the popular leader Pasquale Paoli (for whom Buttafuoco worked) and was temporarily successful. The prospect of independence – and Rousseau's testified support for the Corsicans – made him an obvious choice for a people in search for a constitutional engineer. The situation was, on the face of it, much the same in Poland.

In 1771 Rousseau was asked by Count Michel Wielhorski (an otherwise completely undistinguished Polish nobleman) to present a similar proposal for Poland following the accession to the throne of Stanislaw II, one of Catherine the Great's former lovers.[4] Wielhorski had been requested to seek information about the constitution by members of the *Confédération of the Bar* (a group of Catholic noblemen) who had revolted against the King in 1768. The Confederation was intent on winning Polish independence from Russian influence and sought advice as to how they could establish a political system to that effect (Cranston 1997: 177).

We would have expected that Rousseau (a man fascinated by Solon and Romulus) would have been thrilled to follow in the footsteps of Plato, Hobbes, Machiavelli and other colleagues who – albeit unsuccessfully – had advised politicians on constitutional affairs. While Rousseau claimed to be excited about the project,[5] it is conspicuous that he is strangely unenthusiastic in his autobiographical recollections of the projects. In *Rousseau juge de Jean-Jacques: Dialogues*,[6] the most ruthless and colourful of his four *texte autobiographique*[7] he notes simply – and without affection, that in 1771 'Jean-Jacques devoted six months ... first to studying the constitution of an unhappy nation [Poland], then to propounding his ideas on improvements that needed to be made in that constitution' ('*employé six mois dans le même intervalle a l'examen la constitution d'une Nation malheureusse qu'à proposer ses idées sur les corrections à faire a cette constitution*') (I: 836). He was scarcely more enthusiastic about his work on Corsica's constitution. Reflecting on the invitation by Buttafuoco in *Les Confessions* he simply asserts that the undertaking of writing a constitution for Corsica 'was beyond my strength' (Rousseau 1992: 287). This might explain why he never published the two treatises and, indeed, failed to even finish *Projet*.

The fate of the two treatises may also owe much to the political develop-ments which led to Rousseau's invitations. Corsica – while technically a dependency of Genoa –was de facto a free country when Buttafuoco invited Rousseau to legislate. This, however, was to change. At the end of the Seven Years' War, France had made an agreement with Genoa, as the titular possessor of Corsica, to be allowed to install garrisons at various posts on the Corsican coast. These would eventually be ceased to France. In 1769 Corsica was annexed by France. This development dissuaded Rousseau from concluding his essay.[8] Disappointed – and with a touch of paranoia (he even believed that France had intervened as a personal vendetta against himself) – Rousseau abandoned the *Projet*, as rule by Paris would make it impossible to '*former la nation pour la gouvernement*' (III: 901). Poland was to suffer a similar fate. It is rather remarkable, therefore, that only a couple of years later he embarked on a similar project there, as he knew that the country was in grave danger of being invaded. In *Considérations* – foreshadowing Fichte[9] – he asserted that it was the threat of foreign invasion that made it imperative to try to 'form a nation'. In *Considérations* he writes, 'You cannot possibly keep them [the Russians] from swallowing you; see to it at least that they shall not be able to digest you. Whatever you do your enemies will crush you a hundred times before you have given Poland what it needs in order to be capable of resisting them' (III: 959). This fear of an invasion was warranted – Poland was divided (for the first time) in 1771.

Rousseau and modern definitions of nationalism

That Rousseau encouraged the Poles and the Corsicans to develop strong cultural institutions to defend themselves against greater powers does not make him a nationalist in the modern sense. To render the conclusion that Rousseau developed a doctrine of nationalism hinges on the premise that Rousseau's theory is consistent with commonly recognised and contemporary definitions of nationalism. There are an abundance of theories of nationalism: Hobsbawm (1991), Smith (1988), Kedouri (1960), Anderson (1981) and Gellner (1983), for example. The following analysis is based on Gellner's definition of nationalism, as this has acquired a paradigmatic status (Hall 1998: 1).

Ernest Gellner has defined nationalism as 'a political principle, which holds that the political and national unit shall be congruent' (Gellner 1983: 1). It is about 'entry to, participation in, and identification with a literate high culture, which is co-extensive with the entire political unit' (15). Nationalism is the embodiment of the new imperative of cultural homogeneity, which is the very essence of nationalism for the first time in world history a high culture becomes the pervasive and operational culture of an entire society.

The question is whether Rousseau developed the case for a political order based on cultural homogeneity and 'participation in, and identification with a literate high culture'? It is well known that Rousseau on several occasions advocated the necessity of establishing cultural homogeneity. In *Lettre à D'Alembert* (Rousseau 1758, Bloom 1960) he stressed the necessity of creating political and cultural cohesion through sports, games and national education (a view which also features prominently in *Considérations sur la gouvernement du Pologne* and in *Projet de Constitution pour la Corse*. However, these efforts at creating 'cultural homogeneity' do not make him a nationalist in the strict sense, i.e. as defined by Gellner. Rousseau's considerations in the 1750s were – or, so it might be argued – mostly (un)original elaborations of the doctrine of civic virtue and patriotism developed by Nicolo Machiavelli, in *Discoursi*,[10] and more recently by Pufendorf and Montesquieu. Pufendorf had argued that 'without religion no society can be maintained' (Hendel 1934: 221), a view, which Montesquieu had supported in *L'esprit des Lois* (Book 25, ch. 9). Machiavelli held Christianity responsible for the demise of that patriotism which he deemed necessary for maintaining a healthy republic. The Christian religion had – argued Machiavelli – preached subordination. Its ideas were based on 'humility, abnegation and contempt for mundane things', whereas for 'the Pagan religion the highest good [had been] magnanimity, bodily strength and everything that [was] conducive to make men very bold'. In other words, Christianity had 'made the world weak' and had 'handed it over as prey to the wicked' (Machiavelli quoted in Virolli 1988: 174). Rousseau accepted the thrust of this analysis, yet he was – as we shall see – unwilling to adopt Machiavelli's anti-clerical conclusions.

There is nothing surprising in this lack of originality – from the point of view of traditional nationalism theories. Nationalist sentiments – it is often argued (Hobsbawm 1992) – were simply not connected with political ideas before the Napoleonic wars. Indeed, as Benedict Anderson has noted, the very word 'nation' 'did not come into general usage until the end of the nineteenth century ... if Adam Smith conjured with the wealth of nations he meant by that no more than societies' (Anderson 1981: 4).

Anderson was, perhaps, correct in stating that the nation means no more than societies in Rousseau's early works. Rousseau did not attach political meaning to the word as it was used in *Discourse pour des artes et des sciences* (Rousseau 1750) and in *Discourse pour l' économie politique*[11] (Rousseau 1755). Yet, Anderson was incorrect in stating that the word nationalism was used infrequently. Rousseau, in fact, used the word half a dozen times in the short treatise *Discourse sur l'économic politique*. Moreover, there is a world of difference between the way Rousseau used the term in his early writings, and the way in which he used the word in his mature work; in *Du Contrat Social*, in *Considérations sur la gouvernement du Polonge* and in *Projet de Constitution pour la Corse*.

The core elements of Rousseau's theory of nationalism

While Rousseau may not have developed a 'complete and rounded theory' in his early writings, he arguably developed a doctrine of 'identification with' a culture 'which is co-extensive with the entire political unit' in his later writings. Writing about the risks facing the Polish people he stressed the imperative of shaping their, 'minds and hearts in a national [sic] pattern that will set them apart from other peoples, that will keep them from being absorbed by other peoples and ensure that they remain patriotic' (III: 960). He continued: 'How can we move hearts, and get the fatherland and its towns loved? Dare I say it? With childrens' games; with institutions which appear trivial in the eyes of superficial men, but which form cherished habits and invincible attachments' (III: 955).

Rousseau was not, in other words, stressing that a 'literal high culture' was necessary for creating 'cultural homogeneity', yet his view was still – at least on closer inspection – closer to Gellner's than one might initially suspect, especially because of his emphasis on education.

Under nationalism the state has not merely a monopoly of legitimate violence, but also the accreditation of educational qualifications. Rousseau was in agreement with Gellner on this point. Writing about education in *Considérations,* he wrote: 'Here we have an important topic. It is education that you must count on to shape the souls of the citizens in a national pattern, and so direct their opinions, their likes, and their dislikes that they shall be patriotic by inclination, passionately, of necessity' (III: 966). Yet education was not enough. Like Herder,[12] Rousseau stressed that the instruction of the pupils of necessity should be in their own language. Rousseau was adamant that he 'would not want to have children pursue the usual course of studies under the direction of foreigners and priests'(III: 966). The pupils should, for the sake of homogeneity, 'learn to read literature written in their own country' (III: 966).

The perceived need of establishing cultural homogeneity was not only developed in *Considérations.* Indeed, he outlined a similar argument in *Lettre à D'Alembert* (as noted above). What was new in the later writings was that he explicitly linked this need for cultural unity to national character and not, as earlier, to patriotism and civic virtues. While the early Rousseau stressed – in the *Discourse on Political Economy* – that we must begin by making men virtuous by 'making them love their country' (III: 255), the later Rousseau, no less interested in patriotism, cast this doctrine in nationalist terms. In *Project du Corse* he thus stresses that while 'establishing a nation is undoubtedly useful [he] knows an even more useful [strategy for maintaining cultural homogeneity] and that is establishing a nation for the government' (III: 901). Incidentally, a view which is strikingly close to Massimo d'Azeglio's utterance – following the Italian Risorgimento, that 'we have made Italy, now we have to make Italians' (Azeglio quoted in Hobsbawm 1990: 44).

A civic profession of faith

This doctrine can be traced back to 'On Civic Religion' in Book IV, Chapter VIII of *Du Contrat Social*. 'On civic religion' has puzzled Rousseau scholars (Wokler 1995: 82). The chapter was added to the final manuscript *after* Rousseau had submitted it (Levine 1976). This has been seen as an indication of Rousseau's inconsistency. Having written a radical – even revolutionary – account of political right, Rousseau succumbed to a medieval conception of political right founded upon religion. Whether this is correct remains disputed.[13] Whatever Rousseau's reasons for not including the chapter in the first submission might have been, he had included the chapter in the first draft of *Du Contrat Social,* the *Geneva Manuscript.* This, however, does not resolve the problem. The chapter still seems out of place. Rousseau's credentials as a defender of faith are legion – even if his religious views were controversial. Rousseau, alone among the major thinkers of the Enlightenment,[14] defended Christianity, most famously in the *Professions of faith of the Savoyard Vicar* – the celebrated part of *Emile* (Rousseau 1762) – in *Lettres écrites de la montange* (Rousseau 1764) (where he defended himself again the Genevan authorities condemnation of *Emile*), and in *Lettre a Voltaire* (1756). What is perplexing is that Rousseau, at the very time when he authored these treatises supporting Christianity, denounced Christianity as a civic religion in *Du Contrat Social*.

Unable to solve the riddle Rousseau scholars have read the chapter on civil religion as a competent -if unoriginal – rehearsal of Machiavelli's considerations in *Discorsi* (Virolli 1988: 175). This is a sober and plausible interpretation. Machiavelli was revered by Rousseau and was frequently quoted as an authority (Virolli 1988: 174). There is undoubtedly some truth in this interpretation. Moreover, Rousseau was a philosopher with a taste for paradoxes and contradictions (Bloom 1987: 579).[15] In the words of Allan Bloom, 'Rousseau's thought has an extremely paradoxical character, seeming at the same time to desire contradictories – virtue and soft sentiment, political society and the state of nature, philosophy and ignorance' (Bloom 1987: 559). Rousseau was aware of this. As he wrote in *Du Contrat social*, 'Please attentive reader, do not hasten to accuse me of contradiction. I cannot avoid a contradiction of words, because of the poverty of the language' (III: 373). The limits of his language were *not* – to paraphrase Ludwig Wittgenstein's *Tractatus* (Wittgenstein 1984: 1) – the limits of his world.

However, the question is whether there is a paradox in Rousseau's writings on civic religion. The dominant interpretation cannot explain why Chapter VIII is full of pious references to the 'eternal truth of the Gospels'. An alternative interpretation could, therefore, be that Rousseau, rather than seeking to establish a modern variant of Machiavelli's civic religion of the Romans, seeks to establish a functional equivalent, which can substitute civic religion, and that this functional equivalent is what later becomes his doctrine of nationalism.

Rousseau argues that 'no state has ever been made without a religious basis' (III: 464). However Rousseau, the lamenter of modernity and secularism (c.f. the *Discourse sur les sciences et les arts*), concedes that a civic religion 'can be no longer' (III: 469). Christianity, the only credible candidate, has ruled itself out. Not because he is opposed to Christianity – which he calls 'a holy, sublime and real religion' ('*sainté. Sublime, véritable*') (III: 465) – but because its teaching of a kingdom of another world makes it unsuitable as a means of achieving political cohesion, which is the *raison d'être* of a civic religion: 'the Gospels set up no national [sic] religion' (III: 467). This is not a wholly original interpretation. Pierre Bayle, the seventeenth-century lexicographer, expressed the same view:

> They [the Christians] would have a conscience too delicate to make use of the thousand ruses of politics without which one cannot parry the blows of his enemy ... Do you want a nation strong enough to resist its neighbours? Then leave the maxims of Christianity as themes for the preachers; keep them for theory; and bring your practice under the laws of nature, which will permit one to render blow for blow' (Bayle 1984: 360–6)

However, while Bayle had correctly acknowledged that Christianity was an inadequate civic religion (like Machiavelli before him had done) he had, again like Machiavelli, failed to put anything in its place.[16] Bayle's view was based on *realist* power politics and *Machtpolitik*. Rousseau was certainly not opposed to realist thinking – far from it[17] – however he did not believe that *high politics* could create cultural homogeneity, hence the necessity of a civic profession of faith that differed from Christianity. Traditional society (such as depicted in *La Nouvelle Heloïse*) had ceased to exist and, as a result, a new sense of belonging had to be established; an imagined community based on an abstract (organic) solidarity.[18]

Hobsbawm hints at the same interpretation in *Nations and Nationalism after 1780* (Hobsbawm 1990), but does not pursue the argument. In his words:

> Even when the state as yet faced no serious challenge to its legitimacy or cohesion, and no really powerful forces of subversion, the mere decline of older socio-political bonds would have made it imperative to formulate and inculcate new forms of civic loyalty (a civic religion to use Rousseau's phrase), since other potential loyalties were now capable of political expression. (Hobsbawm 1990: 85)

In other words, *realpolitik* was an insufficient reason for replacing religion.

However, Rousseau's theory is more than a proto-nationalist theory. It fits into his general philosophy – and resolved an apparent contradiction. The civic profession of faith resolves two problems facing Rousseau. It provides him with a mechanism for maintaining 'social homogeneity', and it allows him to maintain his Christian beliefs – even if Christianity is an inadequate civic religion. By introducing the 'civic profession of faith' he relieves Christianity from the burden of being a civic religion – something that this religion is incapable of being.[19] By introducing a secular civic religion he can recast Christianity as a religion, which is 'confined to the internal cult of the supreme God and the eternal obligations [which] is the religion of the Gospels' (III: 469).

What is needed to acquire that societal unity, patriotism and those civic virtues which are necessary for the maintenance of a healthy society, is not a metaphysical creed but a civic 'cult with love of laws', which teaches the citizens 'that service done to the State is service done to a tutular god (III, 465). The alternative to Machiavelli's religious cult is secular version of the same, that is, a 'purely civic profession of faith of which the sovereign should fix articles, not exactly as religious dogmas, but as social sentiments without which man cannot be a good citizen' (III: 468). This doctrine manifests itself in a state where to 'die for one's country becomes ... martyrdom' (III: 465). There is evidently, a link between this view of patriotism as martyrdom and that developed in *Projet de Constitution pour la Corse* where he crafts an oath a allegiance to the nation which involved this: ' I join myself – body, goods, will and all my powers – to the Corsican nation; granting her the full ownership of me, myself and all that depends upon me. *I swear to live and die for her*' (III: 943, italics added).

Rousseau does not, therefore, contradict himself. In fact, his development of a civic profession of faith allows him to have his cake and eat it. It allows him to follow Machiavelli in stressing a need for a civic religion – albeit in Rousseau's case a secular one – and it enables him to maintain his defence for Christianity as an inner religion. By doing the latter he is even able to take a swipe at organised religion, which he loathed (Wokler 1995: 81). Disqualifying Christianity as an inadequate civic religion in favour of a 'civic profession of faith' leaves room for 'the religion of man or Christianity – not the Christianity of to-day, but that of the Gospel, which is entirely different ... all men being children of God recognise one another as brothers' (III: 465).

Faced with the problem of social cohesion in *Du Contrat Social* he turned to the need for establishing a 'national religion in order to safeguard its claim to absolute obedience from the citizen' (Kendal 1985: xxxiii). In *Considérations* and *Projet* he abandons the reference to religion and replaces it with the word nation. This move is first detected in the introduction to *Projet de Constitution pour la Corse*, where he, while recognising the importance of political institutions, stresses that it is impossible to establish a viable political system unless it is based on cultural homogeneity: 'the wise man, observing the due relations, forms the government to suit the nation (III: 901). Thus while 'a thousand clogs and checks are invented for arresting its [the state's] decay ... if they do not tend towards its fall, neither [do they] make any way towards fulfilling its end' (III: 901). All this, writes Rousseau, comes from 'the separation of two things which are inseparable, namely the body which governs and the body which is governed' (III: 901). This sentence might at first be read as a familiar – though often overstated – defence of direct democracy. However, the continuation indicates otherwise, as Rousseau stresses that the key to establishing the congruence between governors and the governed is to found a nation to suit the government – to establish cultural homogeneity, to use Gellner's terminology. If the government is formed to suit the nation then the two actors (governors and the governed) will maintain in balance and any 'change that takes place in one will take place in the other, and the nation, drawing the government with its own weight, will preserve the government as long as it preserves itself'. It is on the basis of this that he can conclude that the 'first rule, which we have to follow is, that of national character. Every people have, or must have, a character. If it lacks one, we must start by endowing it with one' (Rousseau 1962: 335). Yet, how to do this is a question which he only touches upon in *Projet de Constitution pour la Corse* (ostensibly because the Corsican people were in the fortunate condition ('*l'hereux état*') that they already had a nation (Rousseau 1962: 307). For a more elaborate treatment of how to establish a nation we must turn to *Considérations*.

We have already quoted Rousseau's views on the importance of education in shaping the nation. Yet Rousseau – as also alluded to – does not see education as the sole mechanism for creating cultural homogeneity. What makes Rousseau interesting as a nationalist theoretician – especially for readers at the beginning of the twenty-first century – is that he persistently emphasises the integrative effects of mass culture, such as sport and games (III: 955). While Rousseau closely follows Gellner's definition of nationalism in stressing the need for cultural homogeneity he parts company from Gellner is advocating a nationalism, which is based upon a low culture rather than *solely* on a literate high culture. Writing about this theme he finds it indispensable that the Poles 'create games, festivities and ceremonies, all peculiar to your court to such an extent that you will encounter nothing like them in any other country' (III: 962). As an example of how this might be achieved he suggests Spanish bullfights. 'Look at Spain, where the bullfights have done much to keep a certain vigour alive in the people', he writes, before going on to suggest that 'competitions in horsemanship' could have much the same effect in Poland, as they would be 'well-suited to the Poles and would lend themselves to a spectacular display' (III: 963).

What is remarkable in Rousseau's theory is that he – unlike Fichte and Herder – recognises that nationalism is, or can be, manufactured, and indeed must be established to ensure social cohesion, but that this must be done in a way which ensures public participation.

Moreover, and equally important, Rousseau shows that states do not merely succeed because of well-crafted constitutions and institutional frameworks. The dynamics of mens' actions, he argues, lies in the sense of belonging to a community. In an age where the political importance of small communities has evaporated they must acquire this indispensable sense of belonging through a national community – an 'imagined community' to use Anderson's phrase (Anderson 1981). This is not to say that institutions are unimportant, but these are, according to Rousseau, subordinate to – and dependent upon – the sense of belonging to a community. What is of crucial importance, therefore, are institutions and processes which engender this sense of belonging to the imagined community of the nation. This is exactly what Rousseau does in *Considérations* – as usual by using the example of the ancients:

> All the legislators of the ancient times based their legislation on these ideas. All three [Moses, Numa and Lycurgus][20] sought ties that would bind the citizens to the fatherland and to one another. All three found that they were looking for in distinctive usages, in religious ceremonies that invariably were in essence exclusive and national (see the closing paragraphs of *Du Contrat Social*), in games that brought the citizens together, in exercises that caused them to grow in vigour and strength and developed their pride and self esteem; and in public spectacles that, by keeping them reminded of their forefathers' deeds and hardships and virtues and triumphs, stirred their hearts, set them on fire with the spirit of emulation, and tied them tightly to the fatherland. (III: 958)

Excursus: the decline of social capital

Nationalism has had a lot of bad press lately – and rightly so. In the twentieth century millions of people were victims of nationalist hatred. Was Rousseau wrong to advocate this doctrine? Possibly, if he had defended ethnic nationalism – of the racist *blood and soil* variant. Yet Rousseau supported another and rather different variant of nationalism; a civic nationalism – not an ethnic nationalism (Fetscher 1960: 179).[21] Nationalism can be an evil if it degenerates into ethnic strife – yet it can also be a force for good if it is used as a mechanism for creating cultural homogeneity. Rousseau was not alone in thinking this. The great French writer Alexis de Tocqueville reached the same conclusion in *Democracy in America*:

> In order that society should exist and, *a fortiori*, that society should prosper, it is necessary that the minds of all citizens should be rallied and held together by certain prominent ideas; and that this cannot be the case unless each of them sometimes draws his opinions from a common source and consents to accept certain matters of belief already formed. (Tocqueville 1945: 9)

It was these 'opinions from a common source', these 'matters of belief already formed', which laid at the heart of Rousseau's case for nationalism and his adamant insistence that no society could exist without a common culture. Like Tocqueville a century later, Rousseau knew that no society could survive without a common purpose and a feeling among its members that they belonged together and had responsibilities for each other:

> It is national institutions which form the genius, the character, the tastes, and the morals of a people, which make it be itself and not another, which inspire in that ardent love of the fatherland founded upon habits impossible to uproot, which cause it to die of boredom among other peoples in the midst of delights of which is deprived in its own. (III: 960)

Once forged, this sense of belonging to the same community would have tangible effects – Rousseau *inter alia* believed that the crime rate would fall if the citizens where overwhelmed by patriotism: 'they would refrain from picking people's pockets and handing over large amounts of money to scoundrels' (III: 961). However, the feeling of 'being tied to the fatherland' (III: 961), would not be possible if the citizens were but passive observers of, for example, 'plays that are full of talk about nothing by love and historic ranting' (III: 961). This disdain for theatres (which was also the main theme in *Lettre à M. d'Allembert*) may seem slightly odd – and sociologically implausible. Theatre cannot be a harmful form of entertainment – or so we seem to think today. However, substitute the word 'television' with the word 'theatre', and Rousseau's diatribe begins to make sociological sense.

Robert Putnam, an American social scientist, recently published a study which showed that America's 'social capital' – what we could call 'mores', common bonds, or sense of belonging – is at an all-time low, in large measure because of television. Americans are increasingly becoming disconnected from their communities and social structures. This, Putnam showed, had led to lower educational standards, an increase in the number of teenage pregnancies, lower political participation and higher crime rates. Putnam not only agreed with Rousseau – whom he cited (Putnam 2000:

404) – that the forging of social capital would relieve the community from social ills, he also shared Rousseau's misgivings about passive entertainment. Not the theatre but rather its modern-day equivalent, television, was to blame for the malaise: 'television is not merely a concomitant of lower community involvement, but actually the cause of it. A major effect of television's arrival was the reduction in participation in social, recreational, and community activities among all ages' (Putnam 2000: 236). Rousseau seems to have been thinking along the same lines when he, 242 years earlier, wrote, '[Passive entertainment] would serve to destroy the love of work … render people inactive and slack, prevent the people from seeing the public and private goals with which it ought to busy it self' (Rousseau 1960: 64). There is nothing new under the sociological sun.

Duty to the nation?

'Our first duty is to the nation, the second to the one who governs it.' Thus says Lord Bomston in *La Nouvelle Heloïse* (Rousseau 1968: 139). It seems no coincidence that Rousseau lets one of his fictional characters utter this starkly nationalist sentence in the middle of the eighteenth century – decades before nationalism is said to have been developed (Kedouri 1960: 1). Considerations about state and nation were coherently integrated into his oeuvre. Rousseau – arguably the main social theorist in the eighteenth century – is thus not only the main theorist of popular sovereignty, but also a theoretician of nationalism. Rousseau proves that nationalism did exist before the nineteenth century, even by a modern definition (such as that developed by Gellner). Rousseau developed a theory of society based on cultural homogeneity and 'participation in, and identification with culture' as well as he evidently sought to establish a political culture (based on national sentiments), which were 'co-extensive with an entire political unit' – as required by Gellner's definition. Realising the inadequacy of Christianity as a civic religion he developed a doctrine about 'entry in, participation in, and identification with' a 'civic profession of faith' based on patriotism and cultural norms. This doctrine was later developed into a proper nationalist doctrine in Considérations. This conclusion thus falsifies Kedouri's thesis that nationalism was 'invented' in the nineteenth century.

Through his nationalist doctrine Rousseau succeeded in establishing a modern equivalent of the doctrine of patriotism, as well as finding a place for (what he saw as) true Christendom. This is no mean accomplishment.

This conclusion should be ample proof that Benedict Anderson's conclusion regarding nationalist political theorists was premature. At least one major philosopher has developed a political theory of nationalism; namely Jean-Jacques Rousseau. Not everybody will see this as an accomplishment. Rousseau's enthusiasm for nationalism is not in vogue today. Yet it is worthwhile to remember that Rousseau was not the only one to reach this conclusion. A respected and revered – liberal – thinker like John Stuart Mill concurred, noting that 'free institutions are next to impossible in a country made up of different nationalities (Mill 1861, 427). We do not have to agree with these masters; but they challenge our set ways. And we owe them a response in an age where rejection of the multiethnic society is deemed politically 'incorrect'.

Towards an ever closer union?
Rousseau, European integration and world government

Tout ça change mais plus c'est la même chose – at least in international politics. When politicians in the wake of the Second World War devised plans for a federal European super-state to prevent wars, they were not the originators of that idea. In the eighteenth century Abbé de Saint Pierre – a French writer with a poor reputation (Vaughan 1962: 359) – had developed the same idea. Saint-Pierre's plan would hardly have warranted a footnote in the history of ideas had it not been for Rousseau's interest in the project – or rather the interest that Rousseau was urged to take. In the *Confessions* Rousseau recollected

> After my return from Geneva ... through the invitation of Madame Dupin [I was invited to work on the writings of de Saint-Pierre]. These works contained some excellent things, but so badly expressed that it was a wearisome undertaking to read them ... I did not confine myself to the part as translator ... I myself was often on the point of relinquishing it [the work on Saint-Pierre's writings], if I could have drawn back with decency. (I: 407)

This fading enthusiasm is perhaps understandable as Rousseau came to realise how much his own views differed from those of Saint-Pierre. In undertaking the project, Rousseau did not merely re-write the plan to do one of his female friends a favour (and he had a soft spot for women). He had, in fact, taken a long interest in international affairs and the problems of peace – and especially in the problem of creating the latter.[22] In *The State of War* (1755–56) he had written eloquently and disturbingly about war:

I lift my eyes and look into the distance. There I see fire and flames, a countryside deserted, villages pillaged. Monstrous men, where are you dragging these poor creatures? I hear the dreadful noise, such uproar, such screams! I draw near. I bear witness to a murderous scene, to ten thousand slaughtered men, the dead piled together, the dying trampled by horses, everywhere the sight of death and agony. All is the fruit of peaceful institutions. Pity and indignation rise up from the depth of my heart. (III: 609)

A vivid and horrifying spectre such as this was bound to leave a lasting impression on a sensitive man. And Rousseau did not live at a time of peace. From 1740 and onwards the main powers of Europe were at war for fifteen out of twenty-three years. These wars solved nothing – but killed hundreds thousands of people (Hampson 1968: 174). The War of Austrian Succession (1740–48) failed to settle the colonial rivalry, nor did the Seven Year War (1756–63). Not only did the horrors of war prompt him to philosophise, it also gave him the impetus to devise a plan for eradicating it.

Rousseau – unlike Hobbes – did not regard man as evil in himself. The state of nature was not, argued Rousseau, a state of war, still less the nasty, short, brutish and mean existence depicted by the Wiltshireman. Whereas Hobbes' realism was comparable to that of Morgenthau, Rousseau's was closer to the *realpolitik* of Kenneth Waltz (Waltz 1959: 186). Rousseau believed that wars were created by a rivalry between states, not as a result of human nature. 'The war', he wrote in one of his Fragments, 'is not a relation between men, but between states, and here the individuals are only enemies by coincident, and less as citizens than as soldiers' (III: 345). As Christine Jane Carter wrote in *Rousseau and the Problem of War*,

> What Rousseau wishes to establish is that whilst war has its origins in conflict amongst individuals, such conflict does not in itself constitute war, which is only 'natural' among states. For only in war do we see men fighting each other for reasons, which they scarcely know or understand; not as personal enemies but as representatives of the state. It is precisely this, which Rousseau wants to make fully explicit, in the hope that to expose war as the confrontation of artificial bodies will eliminate the persistent idea that it is natural. (Carter 1987: 110)

It is not difficult to find evidence for this interpretation. 'The state of war', wrote Rousseau in *Du Contrat Social*, 'cannot arise from simple personal relations' (III: 357).

As always fascinated by paradoxes – ('I would rather be a man of paradoxes than a man of prejudices', he wrote in *Emile* (II: 82)) – he noted the tragic irony that states which had been established to avert civil wars gave rise to international wars. As he put it in *The State of War*, 'we see men united by an artificial concord, assemble to slaughter one another, and all the horrors of war arise from the efforts made to prevent them' (III: 603). Rousseau's immediate solution – though hardly philosophically spectacular – was the establishment of a mechanism for protecting civilians (what international lawyers call *the doctrine of non-combatant immunity*). While this proposal falls short of the grandeur of utopian ideals – such as presented by Kant in *Zum Ewigen Frieden* – it is testament to the power of political ideas that it was Rousseau's idea, which (at least indirectly) led to the establishment of international humanitarian law (Best 1980: 56–8).

However, Rousseau's status as an important thinker of international politics does not rest on his input into humanitarian law, but on his work on – and critique of – Saint-Pierre's proposal. And it is important to draw a distinction between editing and critique. In *Projet du paix perpétuelle* (III: 563–93) he neutrally outlined Saint-Pierre's proposal, and in *Jugement sur le projet de paix perpétuelle* he passed his (rather harsh) judgement on the plan which he had edited. This distinction has often been lost on even the most prominent observers. Kenneth Waltz – otherwise a fan of Rousseau – is a case in point. Quoting from a passage in *Projet du paix perpétuelle* (which stresses the need for an international legislature for a federation of all European states), Waltz stresses that 'it is easy to poke holes in the solution offered by Rousseau', and he goes on to ask how this 'federation could enforce its laws on the states that comprise it without waging war against them' (Waltz 1959: 185–6). Good question! Indeed, Rousseau had asked the same question in *Jugement*. Rousseau did not write *Projet du paix perpétuelle*, he merely summarised it – and criticised it. Whether Waltz would have agreed with Rousseau's answer to the question is another matter. Rousseau – like Waltz – found the plan unrealistic. He believed that 'vice, deceit, which so many people use, emerges by it self, yet the common good, which we all benefit from, can only be established by war … eternal peace is at the moment an absurd plan (III: 600).

That Rousseau's thoughts were equated with a policy he disliked – and actively rejected – is hardly new. Further his readers might have been justified in their misperception. *Jugement* was published after his death, whereas *Projet du paix perpétuelle* had been published in 1761 (it was initially intended for publication in the periodical *Le Monde comme il est* in 1760 – but the French censor had qualms about it) (Vaughan 1962: 361–2). The *Projet*, which James Madison described as 'preposterous' and 'impotent' (quoted in Spurlin 1969: 85), was not Rousseau's own, rather it was Saint Pierre's. Its contents are nevertheless interesting as they seem to be a catalogue of the institutions which two hundred years later were established under the Treaty of Rome. The *Projet du paix perpétuelle* would be based on a 'federal government [which] shall unite nations by bonds similar to those which already unite the individual members'. In order for this to happen de Saint-Pierre envisaged the establishment of five institutions: the federation needs; all the important powers of the members; a legislative body; an executive with power to compel obedience to the federation's laws; and a prohibition against withdrawal. Whereas Waltz (wrongly) believed that Rousseau advocated this scheme, the latter in reality found that this plan was 'too good to be adopted' ('*étoit trop bon pour être adopté*') (III: 599).

Rousseau's reasons for rejecting the plan were based on two factors: the nature of international politics and the need for national cohesion. What he did not reject, however, was the principle of federation. The concept of federalism is often – though erroneously – believed to originate in the *Federalist Papers*. It did not. Indeed, it would be more historically accurate to credit Rousseau with the invention of federalism rather than Madison. While a major work on federalism by Rousseau seems to have been lost,[23] there are ample examples of his zest for the principle of federation. Rousseau found that the federal system of government was 'the only one, which combine[d] the advantages of large and small states – as essential to correct the radical vice of modern states; their sheer size' (III: 601). It is not, therefore, accurate to call Rousseau 'an armchair federalist' (Miller 1984: 139). Quite the contrary: it was a central tenet in his most practical work of politics.

In *Considérations sur le gouvernement du Pologne*, he stressed that the Poles should 'make it their business to extend and perfect the federal system of government' (III: 970), as well as stressing that they 'should never lose sight of how important it is for Poland to orient its constitution towards federalism' ('*Ne perdons pas de vue l'importance dont il est pour la Polonge de tourner sa constitution vers la forme féderative*') (III: 986). However, and crucially important in the context of a proposal for a federal state comprising all European states, he rejected the idea of a multinational federation. For a start Europe did not have a common culture. Rousseau – unlike a globalist such as Kant – did not believe that the principle of humanity extended much beyond one's own country. 'It would seem', Rousseau wrote in *Political Economy*, that 'the sentiment of humanity dissipates and weakens as it spreads to the whole Earth ... this inclination in us can only be useful to those concentrated among fellow citizens' (III:

255–6). While Rousseau came to realise that the city state was inadequate, and therefore had to be combined with the nation state, he did not consider a European nation-state possible, simply because the Europeans did not share a common national identity or feeling of sameness. 'It is impossible merge these antagonistic countries: The proclaimed brotherhood of Europeans seems but a caricature, and one which scornfully disguises a mutual hatred' (III: 569). This lack of a common culture was, as we saw in the previous section, a central element in Rousseau's political philosophy. His objection against de Saint-Pierre was in large measure a result of this opposition.

Yet, Rousseau's opposition to the *Projet du paix perpétuelle* was also based on more traditional concerns – concerns which belong to the realm of international political theory. We are prone to forget that Rousseau – for political purposes – equated Europe with the whole world. When Abbé de Saint-Pierre proposed a federation of European states he, in effect, presented the seventeenth-century equivalent of World Government – not merely a forerunner of the European Union. And while Rousseau was favourably disposed towards the goal (i.e. perpetual peace) he considered the means thoroughly unrealistic and even somewhat ridiculous. Writing as a novelist, Rousseau had (at the time that he wrote *Jugement*) presented a caricature of Abbé de Saint-Pierre in his successful novel *La Nouvelle Heloïse*. The main character's uncle is depicted as a sad individual obsessed with international politics and the creation of peace – and as someone whose family life breaks down as a result of his interest in lofty ideals at the expense of the care for his daughter (Shklar 1969: 106). Julie – reflecting her creator's preferences – strongly objects to this character; why not concern yourself with the evil you can alter as opposed to the evil you cannot?

Rousseau's attitude towards de Saint-Pierre moved in the same direction. He saw the laws of international politics – i.e. the quest for power – as a fact of life; something that one could not alter. He consequently found it hard to believe that powers would willingly give up their power in pursuit of the common good. 'For the federation to be established it is important not to forget the vested interests' (III: 595). The chief problem of the plan for international peace was, as earlier mentioned, that its advocates forget that 'all observations of kings, or those who perform their roles, reveal that they are driven by two things, and two things only, to increase power externally and to strengthen their power internally' (III: 592). Consequently, the system proposed by Saint-Pierre – while commendable and altruistic – was a political impossibility as no ruler would be willing to sacrifice his power for the general good. So while he might have envisaged that mechanisms for the protection of humanitarian rights could be enforced, he was unconvinced that public international law could prevent the outbreaks of wars:

> As for what is called international law [*'droit des gens'*] it is certain that, for want of sanction, its laws are nothing but chimeras even weaker than the laws of nature. This latter at least speaks to the heart of individuals, whereas international law, having no other guarantee than their utility to the one who submits to it, are respected only as long as self-interest confirms it. (III: 610)

Power politics, realism and the nation state. These are not the ingredients we normally associate with Rousseau. History throws up strange bedfellows. That Rousseau tends towards a conservative standpoint is not widely acknowledged – yet it is hard to deny, having surveyed his views on European integration and international affairs.

Notes

1 It will be noted that Anderson also ignored two other great nationalist minds, namely Herder and Fichte. Fichte especially is arguably a major philosopher.

2 *Rousseau's theory is acknowledged in Brendan O Leary, 'Ernest Gellner's Diagnoses of Nationalism: A Critical Appraisal', in John A. Hall (ed.), The State and the Nation* (Cambridge: Cambridge University Press, 1998), p. 32.

3 The issue is not mentioned in Jean Starobinsky, *Rousseau: la transparance et l'obstacle* (Paris: plon, 1957), in Judith Shklar, *Men and Citizens. A study of Rousseau's Social Theory* (Cambridge: Cambridge University Press, 1969) or in Robert Derathé, *Jean Jacques Rousseau et la Science Politique de son temps* (Paris: J. Vrin, 1988). The exception to the rule is Robert Derathé, 'Patriotisme et Nationalisme au XVIIIe Siècle', in *L'idée de nation, Annales de Philosophie Politique*, no. 8, 1969. Also Alfred Cobban argued that 'for the appearance of the nation state no political inventor can be given credit or blame … but the fact that he [Rousseau] is the first is undeniable'. Alfred Cobban, *Rousseau and the Modern State*, London: George Allen and Unwin, 1969), p. 100.

4 We do not know why the Poles called upon the *philosophes* (Abbe Mably was also commissioned). The Polish Convention – of which Wielhorski was a member – had no political mandate and no authority to speak on behalf of the country.

5 Lettre à M. Buttaffuoco, 22 September 1764, MS Neuchatel, 7899 (Rough Drafts of Letters I and II).

6 On this autobiography see James F. Jones, *Rousseau's Dialogues: An Interpretive Essay* (Genève: Droz, 1991).

7 These 'textes' include *Les Confessions, Dialogues, Revieries du promeneur solitaire* as well as other *fragments autobiographique.*

8 In *Confessions* he writes – seemingly without irony: 'I was unable to feel perfectly easy or to devote my attention seriously to the proposed work of legislation, until I had convincing proof that it was not a mere joke at my expense'. (XII: 287)

9 J.G. Fichte, *Reden an die Deutsche Nation* (in Helge Grell, *Folkeaand og Skaberaand* (Aarhus: Anis, 1988), p. 21), struck a similar note, stressing that is especially important to build a nation when the country in question has been defeated – or even apolitically annihilated. His *Reden* were written on the backdrop of Germany's defeat to France in the battle of Jena in 1806.

10 On Rousseau's indebtedness to Machiavelli see Maurizio Virolli, *Jean-Jacques Rousseau and the Well-Ordered Society* (Cambridge: Cambridge University Press, 1988).

11 For example on pages 242, 246–8, 253 and 269.

12 On Herder noted 'Die ganze Volksseele geht in der Strache ein und klingt aus ihr wieder', Herder, Ideen zur bestimmung des menschheits, quoted in W. Dobbek, *J.G. Herders Humanititatsideal als Ausdruck seines Weltbildes und seine Personlickeit* (Berlin: Braunschweig, 1949), p. 39.

13 The classical article on this subject is Robert Derathé, 'Le Religion Civil selon Rousseau', in *Annals de la Societé Jean-Jacques Rousseau*, 1959–62. For a more recent study see Gugliemo Forni, 'L'Universalisme religieux de Jean-Jacques Rousseau', in Robert Thiéry (ed.), *Jean-Jacques Rousseau, Politique et Nation* (Paris: Honoré Champion, 2001), pp. 483–503.

14 This opposition to the atheists among *les philosophes* is eloquently expressed in Book III of *Les Revieries du promeneur solitaire*: 'instead of removing my doubts and curing my uncertainties … these ardent missionaries of atheism, these overbearing dogmatists [*'imperieux doqmatiques'*] could not patiently endure that anyone should think differently than them on any subject whatsoever. I often defended myself rather feebly because of my distaste and lack of talent for disputation, but never once did I adopt their dismal teaching (desolante doctrine)'. Rousseau, *Revieries du promeneur solitaire* (Bourdeaux: Larousse, 1997), p. 58.

15 Rousseau's awareness of the paradoxical character of his work is well illustrated in *Lettre à M. d'Alembert*, in Allan Bloom (ed.) *Politics and the Arts. Letter to M. d'Alembert on the Theatre by Jean-Jacques Rousseau* (Glencoe Ill: The Free Press, 1960), p. 131.

16 It is interesting to note that Voltaire – his views on Christianity notwithstanding – insisted that citizens needed a civic religion. See Ronald Ian Boss, 'Rousseau's Civil Religion and the Meaning of Belief: An Answer to Bayle's Paradox', in *Studies of Voltaire and the Eighteenth Century*, Vol. 84, 1971, pp. 123–93. For a more recent – albeit shorter – introduction see John Gray, *Voltaire* (London: Routledge, 1998).

17 See Kenneth Waltz, *Man, the State and War* (New York: Columbia University

Press, 1959), p. 181, in which Rousseau is described as a realist. For a more balanced account of Rousseau's thinking on international affairs see Stanley Hoffman and David Fidler (eds) *Rousseau on International Relations* (Clarendon Press: Oxford, 1991).

18 The Durkheimean term 'organic solidarity is used deliberately. Durkheim was an avid reader of Rousseau and was inspired by his thinking. See Emile Durkheim, *Montesquieu and Rousseau: Forerunners of Sociology* (Ann Arbor: University of Michigan Press, 1970).

19 By relieving Christianity of the burden of being a civil religion, Rousseau – perhaps not surprisingly – followed Jean Calvin. Calvin wrote: 'Let us observe that in man government is two-fold: one spiritual, by which the conscience is trained to piety and divine worship; the other civil, by which the individual is instructed in those duties, which as men and citizens [they] are bound to perform ... The former has its seat within the soul, the latter only regulates the external conduct.' Jean Calvin, *Institutes of Christian Religion* (London: James Clarke & Co., 1949) Part III, p. xix. 15. On Rousseau and Calvin see Rousseau, *Du Contrat Social*, III: 382.

20 Respectively the founders of Israel, Rome and Sparta.

21 Following a short review of this, Fetscher writes: 'It is obvious that Rousseau was in no way ['*keinerwegs*'] the war-mongering nationalist that many critics have claimed'. Fetscher, *Rousseaus politische Philosophie* (Neuwied: Hermann Luchterhand, 1960), p. 179.

22 Other books on Rousseau and international relations include, *inter alia*, J.L. Windelberger, *Essai sur la politique étrangére de Jean-Jacques Rousseau* (Paris: Pichard et Fils, 1900). A more recent work is Grace Roosevelt, *Reading Rousseau in the Nuclear Age* (Philadelphia: Temple University Press, 1990).

23 See G.L. Windelberger, *La République conféderative des petits étates: essai sur le systémede politique étrayére de Jean-Jacques Rousseau* (Paris: Presses Universitaires de France, 1900), chapter 2. However, there is some discussion about that. Patrick Riley (*The Cambridge Companion to Rousseau* (Cambridge: Cambridge University Press, 2001a) is sceptical as regards Rousseau's work. See 'Rousseau as a Theorist of International and National Federalism', *Publius*, vol. 3, Spring Issue, 3–17. See also Fetscher, *Rousseaus politische Philosophie*, p. 178 and Catherine Larrère, 'Fedération et Nation', in Robert Thiéry, *Jean-Jacques Rousseau*.

5

The last of the ancients
the first of the moderns?

Do I contradict myself?
Very well then I contradict myself
(I am large, I contain multitudes)
(Walt Whitman, *Song of Myself*, ll. 1325–7)

In one of his fragments Rousseau spoke of a man who 'was one of the moderns [but] who had an ancient soul' (III: 643). This could have been an epitaph for his many autobiographical statements. Rousseau was a weak and often insecure individual but he was also a man with an astonishing confidence in his literary abilities. As early as in the *Discourse sur les sciences et les arts* he predicted that his essay 'would live beyond its century' (III: 3). And so it did. Approaching the tercentenary of his birth, the Swiss note-copier's works are on the reading lists in sundry faculties all across the academic horizon – from anthropology through music and philosophy to political science and even botany.

Why this continued interest in a man who was 'from childhood to his death but an artisan, a bureaucrat or minor employee just as much as a writer' (Launay 1963: 22)? This question is as easy to ask as it is difficult to answer. A short, adequate – but ultimately unsatisfactory – answer is that he was a genius – though not always a very attractive one. In *Dictionaire de la Musique*, one of his lesser known works, he described a genius almost poetically as:

> He who makes the silence speak, who restates thoughts through emotions, and emotions through subtle allusions, who wakes passions in the depth of the heart … [He who], even when depicting the horrors of death, instils into the heart a feeling of life, which never deserts him. (V: 915)

In his more sublime moments, Rousseau did exactly this. Uniquely for a political thinker, he combined a sharp analytical mind with the poetic sensibility of the composer and the novelist. Rousseau, unlike post-modernists, did not renounce reason but he ceaselessly insisted that the passions ought to be granted their rightful place in the political pantheon. Rousseau, like Plato, recognised that it is multiplicity of the soul and the self which, perhaps more than anything else, characterise *l'homme civil*. His whole philosophical endeavour seems like one long paraphrasing of American poet Walt Whitman's dictum 'I am large. I contain multitudes'. Rousseau insisted that man was large enough to contain paradoxical traits that could not be reconciled. His project was to seek a formula for how the different natures could be made to co-exist without mental torment and social *anomie*.

Being victims of a culture that values specialisation, it is difficult for us to grasp the scale of Rousseau's ambition. Specialists by definition focus narrowly. Modern political theorists have had the rather unfortunate, if understandable, habit of focusing on Rousseau's so-called 'political writings' to the exclusion of his other writings. We cannot, however, fully comprehend his political philosophy until we have grasped its relation to his so-called non-political writings. An understanding of Rousseau requires us to understand, as Geraint Perry puts it, how he sought to find a mechanism for teaching individuals to 'be men, women and citizens' (Perry 2001: 247). More specifically, how to 'create a virtuous circle in which transformed human beings could live in a transformed society in which all could equally enjoy a sense both of self-fulfilment and community with others' (248). The activity of being a citizen is intertwined with that of being a whole individual, an individual who could see the beauty in nature, enjoy music, and at the same time perform the duties of a virtuous citizen. This, of course, was not a unique ambition for a great philosopher. Plato, Kant, Hegel and even Mill (to name but a few) aspired to do the same.

Did Rousseau succeed in his endeavour? He recognised – like Burke – that the advent of Godless materialism was undermining the *moeurs*, and that patriotism and nationalism were necessary and, indeed, commendable doctrines, which could reverse the trend caused by the progressing disenchantment of the world. Yet Rousseau – perhaps unlike so-called contemporary conservatives – was not content with the existing inequalities. He was appalled by the treatment of the poor and the snobbishness and wantonness of the rich. This might make him a hero for the political Left. Yet his political remedy was anything but Jacobin. The cure he proscribed was not redistributive programmes, still less schemes for penalising the rich. Rather his solution was to recapture the lost innocence of mankind through negative education (with the occasional institutional incentive thrown in alongside the pedagogic efforts). Political institutions were necessary, as discussed earlier in this work. Yet, Rousseau never succumbed to the illusion that perfect constitutional arrangements could lead to a perfect society. Nor, indeed, would society be much improved if even the wisest men were to be given the reigns of power. Leadership was but a part of the equation. A good polity required *both* wise rulers and enlightened and virtuous citizens. That is to say, a recognition that there could be no rights without duties, no entitlements without obligations. This realisation was not lost on great men. As Susan Dunn has observed: 'When John F. Kennedy electrified a generation by declaring in his inaugural address in 1961, 'Ask not what your country can do for you, ask what you can do for your country' – Rousseau was speaking to us again – with a Boston accent' (Dunn 2002: 29).

Rousseau – exactly like John F. Kennedy – understood that sacrifice is a necessary part of a working polity. He was never an institutionalist (like Madison or Mill), though he greatly admired Montesquieu. He approvingly cited the latter's observation – from *Considérations sur les causes de la grandeur des Romains et leur décadance* – that 'at the birth of societies it is the legislators who shape the institutions, after that it is the institutions who shape the legislators' (III: 381). (Although he also stressed that institutions were not the only factors to shape the law-makers' actions.) Rousseau also shared – indeed advocated – the view that the rulers should be subjected to checks and balances. Why did believe this? Possibly because he, as a commoner, had been at the receiving end of the tyranny of the property-owning aristocracy. As he wrote to the French king's censor, de Melherbes, in a letter from 28 January 1762: 'I dislike those who rule others, I hate the great class, their coldness, their prejudices, their petty sentiments, and their excesses, and I would hate them even more if I despised them less' (Rousseau in Hendel 1937: 219).

It was, perhaps, for this reason that he offered his own (democratic) unique solution to the age-old problem of *quis custodiet ipsos custodes – who guards the guardians.* He did this by suggesting how referendums could be a democratic check on the encroachment of power by the magistrates and developed a case for a constitutionalism, which was *both conservative and democratic.*

The belief in democracy – in mass man's ability to take responsibility for his own life and his society – was an especially new departure. Voltaire, by contrast, believed that there were 'very few republics on Earth [because] [m]en rarely deserve to govern themselves (Voltaire 1962: 257).[1] Where Locke, Madison and Montesquieu envisaged that the lawgivers should be held in check by second chambers, courts or a federal division of powers (i.e. through non-democratic and elitist schemes), Rousseau (inspired by the political system of his native Geneva) championed the people as the check on the rulers.

Beginning in the *Discourse sur l'inégalité* and the *Discourse on Political Economy*, and continuing in *Du Contrat Social* and *Lettres*, Rousseau pointed to the veto-power of the ordinary citizens as a bulwark against radical changes enacted or proposed by over-eager lawmakers. Recognising that the veto-power of the people – such as it existed in Rome – at all times have been viewed with 'alarm by the leaders' ('*ont été de tous temps l'horreur des chefs*') (III: 428), Rousseau believed that the rulers' opposition to the veto-power of the people was the best proof of the efficiency of this system as a constitutional safeguard (428). Far from advocating direct legislation, Rousseau stressed the necessity of establishing a check on the representatives. He advocated a system 'in which individuals [were] content with sanctioning the laws' (III: 113) – but do not make the laws themselves. These views make it difficult to maintain Riker's view that Rousseau believed 'that by reason of popular participation democratic government embod[ies] the will of the people and cannot therefore oppress' (Riker 1982: 9). Quite the contrary. Rousseau would have had some sympathy for Riker's view – though we would have been alarmed by his rationalism and absurd insistence that politics might be reduced to mathematics and algebra.

Rousseau's trust in natural conservatism provided him with the institutional means of avoiding radical and revolutionary change – something which he (like Burke) detested. He developed these views into a constitutionalist doctrine of gradual reform and piecemeal change, the principles of which were outlined in *Du Contrat Social*, the *Discourse sur l'inégalité*, and given a concrete form in *Lettres écrites de la montagne*. The latter is often – though unfairly – overlooked. For while the latter work is rather lesser known than his more abstract treatises it is worth noting that *Lettres* was deliberately written to demystify his theories. Rather than being a merely apologetic tract, *Lettres* was also a popularised version of thoughts which he had previously expressed in a theoretical language. One could perhaps say that *Lettres* stands in the same relationship to *Du Contrat Social* as Kant's *Prolegomena* stands to his *Critique of Pure Reason*. In *Lettres* Rousseau proceeded through examples rather than through stringent deductive reasoning. The result was a thorough defence of the principles of democratic constitutionalism. In *Lettres* he advocated the principle of checks and balances and expressed unequivocal support of at least one aspect of British constitutionalism, a system which 'offer[ed] a model of a just balance between restrictive powers' (III: 874). Like Montesquieu (whom he revered),[2] Rousseau saw England as a model. He was not (as Burke erroneously believed) an opponent of the British system of government.

Rousseau was aware that his writings could be misinterpreted – there is a high price to be paid for eloquence. Defending himself against the charge raised by Louis-François Trochin, the chief prosecutor of Geneva, he reiterated his support for a balanced constitution. In *Lettres écrites dans la campagne*, Trochin had asked the rhetorical question; 'what point is there to having a government under which the people has an unlimited right to legislate'. Rousseau's answer was simply 'I agree' (III: 875). That is, he agreed that the people's power to legislate directly had to be restricted. But Rousseau – perhaps unwisely given the circumstances – did not restrict himself to agreeing with the prosecutor. Being a thinker he developed a philosophical response to a legal charge. Rousseau showed that the Genevan constitution was *not* consistent with the principle of a balanced government, and hence incompatible with his doctrine as laid out in *Du Contrat Social*. The *Petit Conseil* – the ruling body in the city – was unrestricted in its powers. While opposed to direct and unrestricted democracy (an opposition most clearly stated in the *Dedicace* in the *Discourse sur l'inégalité*), he was equally adamant that unrestricted rule by the elite was unacceptable. Hence, while the British constitution is not at all perfect, it was preferable to the prevailing system in Geneva, as the British constitution was a balanced one – while the Genevan constitution was not (III: 875). At least not in practice, as he had previously thought (III: 809). This philosophical analysis was lost on the prosecutor, who – not surprisingly – did *not* respond in kind. Rousseau's books were symbolically burned in the aftermath of his unsuccessful intervention. This is not the important matter here. What is interesting, from a philosophical point of view, is the thrust of Rousseau's response. As a true philosopher of freedom – albeit of a non-liberal sort – Rousseau praised the English system under which 'no citizen is imprisoned in contravention of the law, his home is sacred' (III: 875). Again this doctrine would have been unoriginal had it not been for Rousseau's (in the true meaning of the word) 'populism'.

In advocating the referendum as an alternative constitutional safeguard he sided with the people – not with the rulers. This is not surprising. Rousseau's position vis-à-vis other philosophers was always that of an outsider, and of a spokesperson of the speechless and underprivileged.

Constitutionalism was never an end in itself for Rousseau. Social justice was the main cause of his indignation. As he wrote in one of his unpublished *Observations*, 'the main source of all evil is inequality' (III: 50). While statistical evidence from the period must be treated with utmost caution there are indications that there was considerable – and increasing – inequality at the time. Less than 2 per cent of the population held one-third of the land. While representing only 5 per cent of the population, the landowners received 50 per cent of the landed capital and almost the totality of the rents from farms, sharecropping, various local taxes and rights of domain of all kinds.[3]

Most other constitutionalists were well-to-do aristocrats (Montesquieu), wealthy bourgeois businessmen and lawyers (Madison), professors (Kant and Hegel) or on the pay-roll of the rich and influential (Locke). Rousseau, the watchmaker's uneducated son, was not. And it showed. His constitutionalism was not driven by a fear of the masses but rather by a distrust of the rich as a class – and a rare trust in the people. He was interested in constitutionalism precisely because he realised that checks and balances were needed to protect the masses against the rich – and because he realised that the existing system did *not* protect the impoverished masses. In the cause of history, wrote Rousseau, 'legal power turned into arbitrary power' (III: 187). While political societies were founded upon a common interest, these commonwealths degenerated as the rich exploited the poor; 'the same vices that [rendered] social institutions necessary, [were] the same which rendered the abuse of these institutions unavoidable' (III: 187). In the absence of checks on the rulers 'political distinctions would necessarily lead to social distinctions [and hence] the inequality between the people and their chiefs' (III: 188).[4] Or as he put it in *Du Contrat Social*:

> Under a bad government … equality is only an appearance and an illusion; it serves only to keep the poor in their wretchedness and sustain the rich in their usurpation. In truth, laws are always useful to those with possessions and harmful to those who have nothing; from which it follows that the social state is advantageous to men only when all possess something and none has too much. (III: 367)

'Everything', wrote Rousseau scholar Jean Starobinsky, 'begins with the experience of social outrage' (Starobinsky 1988: 221). For Rousseau *tout le mal vient de l'inégalite* – inequality is the root of all evil. Rousseau occasionally found it difficult to contain his anger. In a letter to a Mme de Francueil he angrily asserted that 'it is the class of the rich, your class, that steals the bread from my children' (II: 143). Such statements, not surprisingly, have been used by generations of radicals and other proclaimed champions of the downtrodden. And yet Rousseau – as we have noted – did not quite fit the revolutionary bill. While an uncompromising foe of an economic system that sacrificed people for profits, he did not advocate the abolition of private property, still less did he seek to return man to a bygone age of pre-modernism. His economic philosophy – like that of Adam Smith – combined the doctrines of the physiocrates and the mercantilists. Yet, where the Scot combined the physiocrats' zeal for free trade with the mercantilists' aversion against agriculture, Rousseau did the opposite, placing agriculture at the centre of his economic theory – and rejecting the reliance on free trade. His rejection of *laissez-faire* was not, however, merely based on economic considerations. Although more of an economist than often recognised (Fridén 1996), his conclusions stemmed more from ethical beliefs than from considerations concerning profitability. He sought to establish an ethical economic system.

Arthur Schoppenhauer once described Rousseau as 'undoubtedly the greatest moralist of all times' (Schoppenhauer cited in Dent 1991: i). Not entirely accurate if one judges him solely on the less than flattering *autoportrait* in *Les Confessions*, but a philosophically accurate assessment given the thrust of Rousseau's endeavour to challenge modernity and its debauchery of morals. One might (with Alistair MacIntyre) conclude that the moral philosophy of modernity is a catalogue of theories seeking to justify good actions without recognising that goodness exists – clearly an impossibility. The philosophers of modernity have (in vain) sought to develop a theory of the concern for the welfare of others that took self-interest as the unquestionable point of departure. And while Kant deserves credit for showing that any idea of goodness required the *gute Wille* (the good will) as a necessary condition (an action is 'good' only when the individual's intentions are good), Rousseau deserves credit for putting Kant on to his attack on utilitarianism. Kant's categorical imperative would not have been possible without Rousseau. 'For an action to be just', wrote Rousseau, 'it must be so in all its relations.' Eric Weil might have been exaggerating when went as far as saying that 'it took a Kant to think Rousseau's thoughts' (Weil 1952: 3). Yet he arguably had a point. The German's philosophy would have been unthinkable had it not been for Rousseau (Velkley 2002: 18).

While Mandeville, Hobbes, Madison and even – in our day – John Rawls appealed to rational egoism in order to establish a system of common welfare and goodness, Rousseau despised this view. He spoke scornfully of those who 'get an odious pleasure out of seeking for sinister interpretations of everything and of seeing nothing from the good side, not even what is good' (Rousseau 1979: 237), and the Savoyard Vicar attacked what he called a an 'abominable ... philosophy[,] one which is embarrassed by virtuous actions, which [must] fabricat[e] base intentions and motives without virtue' (Rousseau 1979: 283).

He not only rejected that the result of their endeavours could be described as 'good', he also – and more importantly – challenged the description of man as an individual seeking his hedonistic and rational self-interest. The Hobbesian caricature of man was not only morally repugnant, it was also inaccurate. The rational choice theorists from Hobbes onwards have contended that we help the poor for fear that we might find ourselves at the bottom of the social order (Rawls 1971: 79). Rousseau did not reject that individuals sought self-protection (*amour de soi-même*), yet this was not the only impulse that drove them. 'We must not', he wrote in a passage in *Discourse sur l'inégalité*,

confuse selfishness [*amour propre*] with self-love [*amour de soi-même*]; they are two very distinct passions both in their nature and in their effects. Self-love is a natural sentiment, which inclines every animal to look after its self-preservation, and, which guided in man by reason and *qualified by compassion* is productive of humanity and virtue. Selfishness is but a relative and factitious sentiment engendered in society, which inclines every individual to set a greater value upon himself than upon any other man, which inspires men with all the mischief they can do to one another. (III: 219, italics added)

Rousseau's doctrine thus differed radically from the utilitarian and Hobbesian theories, which elevated hedonism, and made a virtue out of vice. While recognising that man sought self-preservation (*amour de soi-même*), Rousseau emphasised that this was 'qualified by compassion' with our fellow men – and that this feeling of *pitié* was completely unrelated to our narrow self-interests. Yet as the proto-Kantian thinker he also was, Rousseau was not content with simply drawing attention to the existence of compassion as a strong motive driving men's actions. He was eager to establish what we (for want of a better expression) might call 'transcendental' conditions for our natural urge to do good. In a famous passage he wrote:

Although compassion [*pitié*] is native to the human heart, it would remain eternally quiescent unless it were activated by imagination. How are we moved by compassion? By getting outside ourselves and identifying with the being that is suffering. We only suffer as much as we can believe him to suffer. It is not in ourselves but in him that we suffer. (V: 395)

Compassion thus became empathy; the ability to step into someone else's shoes and then step out again. Our fellow beings' sufferings warm us and give us a common sense of humanity. But how are we to imagine what it is like to suffer? Are we still capable of feeling compassion in an age and at a time when *amour propre* has the upper hand? Rousseau's answer was negative – but not entirely disparaging. Society – in its bourgeois variant – was an obstacle to our natural goodness. As he wrote in the fragment *Le Bonheur Public*: 'What makes human misery is the contradiction, which exists between our situation and our desires, between our duties and our inclinations, between nature and social institutions, between man and citizen' (III: 510).

Our true self had to be re-awakened (a project he undertook in *Emile*). Through 'negative education' man would, or could, rid himself of the artificial mask of vanity and that unnatural selfishness which had become the hallmark of the society Rousseau despised. Rousseau left no one in doubt that a just and moral society could *not* be re-established except through a concerted effort. Education – public as well as private – was necessary. The *bon sauvage* was no longer. In our age 'we have to develop our social feeling as we become enlightened' (V: 395). Our compassion for other beings thus required education and a 'great deal of acquired knowledge' (V: 395). Not academic knowledge, but knowledge gained through practical experiences and an apprenticeship in the art of life.

Rousseau's educational ideal, therefore, was not totalitarian.[6] Not grounded in a desire to shape man in his own image. Rather, 'negative education' was aimed at rediscovering the individual's natural – but hidden – self. In a sense Rousseau's plan for negative education sought to offer mankind a new beginning. This was necessary as a return to the original state was an impossibility.

Man – as he lived before he was lured into civilisation – was a loner who did not engage in lasting relationships:

> Such was the condition of infant man; such was the life of an animal confined at first to pure sensations, and so far from harbouring any thoughts of forcing her gift from nature, that he scarcely availed himself of those which she offered to him of her own account. (III: 178)

But difficulties soon arose, and 'original man' (Rousseau did not mention women)[7] gradually became engaged with other men, learned to co-operate – and showed compassion for fellow members of his species. Gradually the blissful life in the state of nature that preceded civilisation was somehow broken up and distorted when the rich – through the power of their wealth – usurped power, and relegated their fellow-men to an enslaved existence.

> Such was, or must have been, the origin of society and law, which gave new fetters to the weak and new powers to the rich, irretrievably destroyed natural liberty, fixed forever the laws of property and inequality; changed an artful usurpation into an irrevocable right; and for the benefit of a few ambitious individuals subjected the rest of mankind to perpetual labour, servitude and misery. (III: 178)

The losers were conned into accepting their miserable lot through deception. They lost not only their freedom, but also their sense of direction. Marx, who saw this as clearly as Rousseau (Marx 1977: 121), called it 'alienation' ('*Entfremdung*'). Rousseau too found that man had become an alien; a vain being on a meaningless – and unnatural – quest for *amour propre*. Of course history was not linear. There had been moments when man had – for a short period of time – managed to overcome the predicament of a depraved civilisation, as was the case in the Roman republic, just as there were lacunae of the good (natural) life in the serene alpine villages described in *La Nouvelle Heloïse*. But these were exceptions. As a rough rule civilisation had depraved man, yet – as these examples showed – there was a way out of the misery if man could be taught to live together under a just constitution. Was Rousseau right to think so? Had he found the right cure?

Perhaps both. Perhaps neither. Like Plato, Rousseau later changed his prescribed cure as well as making changes (or at least very significant additions) to this system. The political and educational blueprints (*Emile* and *Du Contrat Social*) were far from identical with his more practical suggestions in *Projet du Corse* and *Considérations sur la gouvernement du Pologne*. Whereas in *Emile* he had been concerned with the private sphere – with private education – the focus in *Projet sur la constitution de la Corse* and *Considérations sur la gouvernement du Pologne* changed to public education. Likewise the rather more institutionalist account in *Du Contrat Social* and *Lettres* gave way to a more nationalist account in the later writings. The common denominator in the latter works was that the establishment of public mores were essential for maintaining a healthy society. This view was one that Rousseau always had held – as one can see from both the *Discourse sur l'inégalité* and *Political Economy* – but in the later writings it took centre stage.

Social injustice, *amour propre*, and the disenchantment of the world; these were the problems that prompted Rousseau to become a writer. The problem for Rousseau was that he – when he came to write his later writings (*Projet sur la constitution de la Corse, Considérations sur la gouvernement du Pologne* and possibly his writings on international relations) – realised that the situation was *worse* than he had hitherto expected, and that he had overlooked other causes which further weakened the society of men.

Rousseau lived at a time of rapid social and economic change. The only constant in modernity is change, but not all thinkers have realised this. Rousseau, like Marx and Hegel, was a thinker who was aware that he was living in the world of radical transformation. World history is dynamic, yet can only be described in static terms. Rousseau, the last of the ancients and the first of the moderns, lived on the threshold of the modern age. His upbringing took place in a static society in a city shaped by the classical republican virtues, and it was these ideals of the small, self-sufficient, societies he initially held up as a model in his political writings. Yet the reality that he increasingly faced was that his model was being made obsolete by large territorial states and an economic system that suited these. Previously Rousseau had noted that *amour propre* and declining patriotism posed a problem even in the model cities. Now he was faced with the problem that the preferred model was vanishing – and with it all the virtues that were to hold society together.

Not all prominent thinkers have taken the consequences of radical change into account. Aristotle – the undisputed chronicler of the ancient city states – chose to ignore the changes that were taking place under his philosophical nose; i.e. his pupil Alexander the Great's conquest of the world and establishment of a world empire that made the city state all but a meaningless concept, and proved that Aristotle's science of politics was past its sell-by date perhaps even before the polymath had penned it. Other thinkers have reacted to momentous changes by making change the central element of their thinking (e.g. Hegel, and perhaps even Plato), still others – and this is where we find Rousseau – have sought to update their philosophies and take account of the momentous changes. In Rousseau's case this updating led – albeit unintentionally – to the establishment of the most successful of all the ideologies of modernity: nationalism.

Poor Jean-Jacques, so often cited, so rarely quoted, so consistently misunderstood. '*C'est la faute à Rousseau*' ('It is Rousseau's fault') said one of the characters in Hugo's *Les Misérables* (Hugo 2000: 313). A bit of an exaggeration – but not widely off the mark. History's verdict has been harsh. Hippolyte Taine and other historians of the French Revolution have

wasted few opportunities to denounce his views. Rousseau is the straw-
man par excellence, the quintessential scapegoat, a literary hate figure who
could always be invoked when a critic was in need of a culprit for the
miseries of modern society. And this is not only true for historians of the
French Revolution. Conor Cruise O'Brien's assessment of the philosopher
is as revealing as it is typical (and ill-informed):

> Rousseau's place in France now appears perennially secure. He simply comes
> with the language. But Rousseau also holds an influential place within the
> English speaking world through the vogue for the 'politically correct' and
> 'multiculturalism' now dominant in certain faculties of several major
> American universities … The malignant magic of the grand charlatan is
> liable to be with us for some time. (O'Brien 2002: 315)

Rarely has an erudite man been more misinformed. Rousseau was many
things; a vagabond, a note-copier, a poet, a composer, a pedagogue and a
political scientist but he was *never* a multiculturalist, and he certainly did
not go along with the liberal secularism of the so-called politically correct.
Of course many 'progressives' have misinterpreted Rousseau (see
Gourevitch 1999 for an overview). Yet these advocates of the Jacobin
interpretation have tended to overlook his later writings, moreover they
have ignored Rousseau's ceaseless profession of his Christian faith, his
opposition to modernity and his support for private property. Indeed,
one wonders which of the great man's works they have read to find support
for their claims.

Rousseau was a compassionate conservative – and he did not believe
that his doctrine was compatible with multiculturalism. His chief political
concern was compassion with the poor –but it was (in his view) impossible
to create the political and moral conditions for helping the poor without
the establishment of a nation state, that is to say without the establishment
of a sense of common solidarity between citizens.

This was a new departure. Communitarian thinkers like Cicero and
Machiavelli had earlier emphasised the necessity of the virtue of patriotism,
the love of the fatherland and the willingness – if need be – to sacrifice
oneself for the commonwealth. Rousseau both shared and went beyond
the aspiration of the ancient masters. As a patriot this *citoyen de Géneve*
never tired of showing how our emotional affection for the fatherland
could produce the most illustrious acts of bravery and self-sacrifice. In *De
la Patrie*, an early fragment, he had pondered 'why it is that the Earth, the
common mother of all people, does not create the same sentiment as that
of the fatherland' (III: 534). However, this patriotism was with the small

community in which everyone knew everybody. The patriots of ancient Sparta sacrificed themselves for people they knew and loved, and whose fate concerned them personally. With the growth of the territorial state (after the Treaty of Westphalia in 1648), sacrifice for the small community was politically meaningless as the small communities had become politically unimportant, and historically obsolete. Nationalism, Rousseau was to suggest, proved to be the solution. Whereas patriotism, as used by Machiavelli and Cicero, was identification with a concrete community, the nationalism proposed by Rousseau was identification with, what Benedict Anderson has aptly described, 'an imagined community'. In Anderson's words, in a nation the political community is 'imagined because the members of even the smallest nation will never know most of their fellow members, meet them, or ever know of them, yet in the mind of each lives the community' (Anderson 1981: 6). Rousseau saw this – and acted upon his newly discovered insight. Yet this is not commonly recognised in the historical overviews of Western political philosophy – nor is it commonly recognised among scholars of nationalism.

Rousseau's place in the intellectual history of nationalism is too rarely acknowledged (Velkley 2002: 32). This is regrettable. The fact is that he – alongside Herder and Fichte – developed a model for: 1) how the emotional attachment to a nation could be generated; 2) how a redevelopment of the ancient doctrine of patriotism could be transformed into a new, powerful doctrine; 3) how this could be done in practice; and 4) how a doctrine of nationalism could perform the functions of civic religion in ancient Greece and Rome.

Rousseau, as already noted, was not the only thinker to develop a case for nationalism. Herder and Fichte are commonly recognised as the founding fathers of this not unproblematic doctrine. Yet the two Germans, unlike Rousseau, were not sociologists. While seeking the same as Rousseau (i.e. social cohesion and solidarity), their case for nationalist sentiments was always clothed in mysterious and metaphysical notions of the *Volksseele* – literally the common soul of the people (an entity that Fichte claimed always had existed). In theoretical speak, the Germans were *pre-mordialists*. Rousseau, by contrast, was a *constructivist* (though a conservative and communitarian one at that). While he recognised that a people might share a common history and ancient myths, he regarded the nation state as an artefact. And it was in order to make this artefact into a vehicle for social cohesion that he suggested how a sense of patriotism could be developed.

It is easy to reject this philosophy as dated or *altmödisch*. Yet it is – political correctness notwithstanding – difficult to claim that states without a common sense of direction and a common set of values have thrived even in the age of multiculturalism. Maybe Rousseau had a point after all. And maybe his true allies are those on the political Right who question the wisdom of secular multiculturalism.

Last thoughts

'A true lawgiver must have a heart full of sensibility. He must fear himself and love mankind.' Edmund Burke penned these words in his *Reflections on the Revolution in France* (Burke 1986: 281). It is indicative of the misperception of Rousseau's philosophical project that these words just as easily could have been written by the very man whom Burke – erroneously – held responsible for all evil emanating from the French Revolution. Recapturing the lost innocence, or rather salvaging whatever was left of it, was Rousseau's aim – just as it was Burke's.

But of course there were differences. Rather than stressing the importance of institutions, Rousseau pointed to 'negative education' as a mechanism, which could and would prevent ingenious schemes of elitist legislation based on rationalistic hubris and misplaced delusions of scientific omnipotence.

As befits a classical thinker, Rousseau's contribution to Western philosophy was rich in detail and even broader in scope. Like other critics of modernity – Kierkegaard and Pascal come to mind – Rousseau's philosophy was a showdown with a society marred by Godless materialism, absurd social inequalities, and unnatural inter-human relations. Men, argued Rousseau, would *not* be set free if left to himself. Liberty, as understood by Rousseau, could only be acquired once *man* – and Rousseau was not gender-neutral – had reconciled his natural, spiritual, and social sides of himself with the requirements of living in an advanced civilisation. Men, argued this most unlikely of thinkers, could only be free when – or if – they recognised the imperatives of living in a family, in a republic and in harmony with a universe created by God: *Vitam impendere vero!*

Notes

1 It should perhaps be noted that Helvétius expressed some sympathy for democracy (not surprising given his views on equality). See Irwing Louis Horowitz, *Claude Helvétius: Philosopher of Democracy and Enlightenment* (New York: Paine-Whitman Publishers, 1954).

2 This reverence is perhaps best illustrated by a letter he wrote to Jean Perdriau

when Montesquieu died: 'You will regret as I do the death of the illustrious Montesquieu. He had no need of so long a life to become immortal; but he ought to have lived for ever to teach people their rights and duties' (III: 277).

3   See Fernand Braudel and Ernest Labrousse (eds), *Histoire Economique et Sociale de la France* (Paris: Presses Universitaires de France, 1970), pp. 139, 476–7.

4   Compare this statement with Burke's observation in *A Vindication of Natural Society*: 'It was observed that men had ungovernable passions, which made it necessary to guard against the violence they might offer to each other. But a worse and more perplexing difficulty arises, how to be defended against the governors? *Quis custodiet ipsos custodes?*' Edmund Burke, *A Vindication of Natural Society*:, in Edmund Burke, *The Works of the Hon. Edmund Burke*, (London: John Nommo, 1887), vol. 1, p. 46.

5   Kant was always unequivocal about his debt to Rousseau. In his *Nachlass* ('Unpublished Writings') – Kant writes 'I am an investigator by inclination. I feel a great thirst for knowledge and an impatient eagerness to advance, also satisfaction at each progressive step. There was a time when I thought that all this could constitute the honour of humanity, and I despised the mob, which knows nothing. Rousseau put me straight. This dazzling excellence vanishes. I learn to honour men, and would consider myself much less useful than common labours if I did not believe that this consideration could give all the others a value, to establish the rights of humanity.' Immanuel Kant, *Fragmente aus dem Nachlässe*, in *Kants Sämtliche Werke* (Leipzig: Leopold Voss, 1868), vol. VIII, p. 624.

6   Fernon has noted: 'communities can no longer be based simply on arrangements in which individuals maximise their desires within a bare legal framework of seeming non-interference, [hence for Rousseau] the cultivation and education of sentiments attain overarching importance' N. Fernon, *Domesticating Passions. Rousseau, Women and Nation* (London: Wesleyan University Press, 1997), pp. 5–6.

7   Of course. Rousseau had plenty to say about women – though not always things which have endeared him to latterday feminists. As Nancy Hirschman has written, 'since feminist political theory began as a subfield … that famous sexist Jean-Jacques Rousseau has been the political theorist that feminists love to hate'. Nancy Hirschman, 'Rousseau's Republican Romance', review article, *Political Theory*, vol. 30, no. 1 (2000), 164. A new approach by feminists is contained in Elizabeth Rose Wingrove's *Rousseau's Republican Romance*. Wingrove reads Rousseau metaphorically, arguing that Rousseau's 'republicanism consists in proper performance of masculinity and femininity'. She goes on to show – so it is argued – that 'republican identity is constructed through sexual identities, and sexual identities through political forms'. See Elisabeth Rose Wingrove, *Rousseau's Republican Romance* (Princeton: Princeton University Press, 2000), p. 6; p. 167. Nicole Fermon also has seen gender as the main theme in his philosophy: 'women, both real

and metaphorical, are at the centre of [Rousseau's] project to reform politics, which for Rousseau means all human relations. Women, for Rousseau … primarily means the mother – the place of repair and consolation, of feeding, of reassurance, that which resist separation(s).' Nicole Fermon, *Domesticating Passions. Rousseau, Woman, and Nation* (Hanover and London: Wesleyan University Press, 1997), p. 4. For a more thorough treatment of the subject the reader may wish to consult: Paul Hoffman, 'Le mythe de la femme dans la pensée de Jean-Jacques Rousseau', in *La femme dans la pensée des Lumières* (Paris: Ophrys, 1977), pp. 359–446; Joel Schwartz, *The sexual politics of Jean-Jacques Rousseau* (Chicago: University of Chicago Press, 1984); Mary Seidman Trouille, *Sexual politics in the Enlightenment: women writers read Rousseau* (Albany: SUNY Press, 1997).

6

Epilogue: in the beginning was song

And the light shineth in the darkness;
and the darkness comprehended it not.

(John 1.5)

We have (rather deliberately) said very little about the subject of music, as this is not obviously a part of Rousseau's social philosophy. Yet music was – though scholars have often forgotten this[1] – Rousseau's main passion, and this passion spilled over into his political writings in more ways than one. Rousseau, the musician and note-copier, was an accidental philosopher. Had he not seen the prize question from the Academy in Dijon on that fateful day in 1749, chances are that Rousseau would have remained an obscure figure and not a celebrated or reviled author. It is more likely that he (at best) would be remembered as a (very minor) composer – though Mozart adored his work (Wivel 1996: 65) In *Dialogues* he has the character of Jean-Jacques say of Rousseau, who is the subject of this strangest of autobiographies; 'he was born for music … he discovered approaches that are clearer, easier, simpler and facilitate composition and performance … I have never seen a man so passionate about music as he' (I: 872–3). This passion prompted his first published work – *Projet concernant de nouveaux signes pour la musique*, which he (without much success) sent to the *Academie des Sciences* in the early 1740s, and his obsession with music was evident in his numerous writings on musicology (*Dictionnaire de musique*, *Lettre sur la musique française* and *L'Origine de la mélodie*) and, of course, in the music he composed.

Rousseau studied music at Le Maître in Annecy, and taught himself by reading and annotating contemporary composers. During his stay in Italy he was captivated by Italian music, and upon his return to Paris in 1745, he completed his first opera, *Les Muses Galantes* (of which only parts have survived). It was after the composition of this work that he fell out with the most notable French composer at the time, Jean-Philippe Rameau. During a rehearsal in the house of La Pouplinière in 1745, Rameau accused Rousseau of having copied some of the opera's passages from an Italian composer. Rousseau never forgave him! Following some difficult years Rousseau finally achieved musical fame in October 1752, with *Le Devin du Village*, first performed for the court in Fortainebleau, and taken up by the *Académie Royale de Musique*. It stayed in the Opera's repertory for sixty years, and the youthful Mozart used the libretto for his *Bastien und Bastienne*. Indeed, Mozart's debt to Rousseau was not only confined to his youthful works, but also to his more mature works. Mozart's biographer Robert W. Gutman has written thus:

> In the *Marriage of Figaro*, Rousseau's principle of the *General Will*, or common good, hovers over the luminous conciliation achieved in the final moments: Count Almaviva's contrition restores harmony to the domain of Aquasfrescas, the characters' sense of well-being derived from the new social contract guiding their relationships one to the other. (Gutman 1999: 123)

Not surprisingly, perhaps, the storyline was a romanticised praise of rustic simplicity. Yet his musical mind was felt in subtler ways than this. 'Rousseau argued that the modern harmonic system depends on an "analytic" and "scientific" way of thinking, which he termed *L'esprit de sistême*' (Blum 1985: 352). This had profound implications for his philosophy. The whole tenor of his prose had a musical aura about it. His works were composed rather than written – which, perhaps, explains his eloquence. Readers of Rousseau's work in the original French have been struck by the rhythmical patterns. Rousseau's prose reads as a melody: 'just as in his musical compositions, in his prose Jean-Jacques knew how to quicken and retard tempo for the sake of emphasis' (McDowell 1968: 19). This musical quality was not unintended. Through the melodious tone he wanted to prove a philosophical point (Wokler 1987: 328). He lamented, in *The Essay on the Origin of Language*, that philosophers, 'in cultivating the art of convincing had lost the art of arousing' (V: 425). Language had lost its potency, and modern man was doomed to live in a state of 'tranquillity like that of the imprisoned companions of Odysseus waiting to be devoured by the cyclop' (V: 425). Without the ability to speak passionately and with arousal, 'we can only groan and be quiet' (III: 609). Music, however, held out some hope, as this was the *only* means through which man could awaken our slumbering emotions. In *Dictionnaire de musique* he wrote that music acts more intimately on us by in a sense arousing in us feelings similar to those, which might be aroused by another … may all nature be asleep, he who contemplates it does not sleep, and the art of the musician consists in substituting for the insensible image of the object that of the movements which its presence arouses in the heart of he who contemplates. (V: 860–1)

Music, in other words, held the key to restoring our original emotions, that natural 'goodness of man', which manifested itself in the natural compassion with suffering, weak and unfortunate individuals. It is, perhaps, indicative that Rousseau – the thinker of natural goodness of man and a composer – never tired of stressing that music and song was man's first impulse (Wokler 1987: 328). The first languages must have been poetic rather than prosaic – they would have been sung rather than spoken. And the significance that came to be 'attached to their terms depended upon the musical forms in which these were constructed' (327). In the *Origin of Languages*, Rousseau wrote: 'The first stories, the first declarations, the first laws were in verse, it had to be so, since passions spoke before reason. The same was true of music. To say and to sing were formerly one' (V: 410–11). Therefore, before men and women began to communicate, and before they succumbed to *amour propre*, they had expressed themselves in an impulsive manner – that is by singing. This theory may be empirically dubious. The claim that language was conceived in musical ebullience seems farfetched as a linguistic hypothesis – and, in truth, it is unlikely that it was ever intended to be one. Yet the argument is metaphorically sound in the context of Rousseau's general philosophy. Just as music gave way to rational discourse, the natural goodness of man was replaced by selfishness and calculation. The sentiments which had once given rise to song were stifled, repressed and forgotten as the social relations of men and women changed under the bondage of an unjust civilisation. There is nothing new in this model, no discrepancy between Rousseau's political theory and his philosophy of music. Rousseau, we must never forget, was writing against the backdrop of the 'disenchantment of the world'. Even music, he believed, was in danger of being swept away by the torrents of scientism and wanton philosophy. Rameau,[2] not only a composer but also a materialist musicologist, had developed an ingenious and elaborate science of music based on Newtonian physics. This was an almost blasphemous position according to Rousseau. In *Lettre sur la musique française*, he wrote, 'If you limit the music to motions [and other physical phenomena], you completely rob it of its moral effects.' Moral effects, which he refers to as the 'voice of nature' (V: 350). As in society in general, music had followed a process of both degradation and progress; it had been given articulation, substance and an intellectual basis. For Rousseau the error of Rameau and his followers was to think that the science of harmony – a branch of physics – could elucidate musical phenomena. In fact, music could not be reduced to a set of vibrations. The underlying sense of music was moral and contingent on the specificity of sensitive beings. For this reason music, as an object of study, was fundamentally different from other art forms. 'Colours', wrote Rousseau, 'are the ornament of inanimate beings; all matter is coloured; the voice proclaims a being endowed with sense; only a sensitive being can sing' (V: 420). No wonder Rousseau was fond of quoting Horats' dictum *sunt verba et voces, praeteraque, nihil* – 'there are words and voices and nothing else' (V: 287).

These utterances are a part of his general philosophy. Rousseau never *just* wrote about music. His writings about music were *also* metaphors for his general *Kulturkampf*, that is, in his struggle against the decay or morals and the advances of Godless materialism. It was Rousseau's central idea that scientism and reason alone could not edify man, let alone awaken his sensible heart.

Music was a countervailing force, a subversive means of undermining the empty castle of rationalism. Music, for Rousseau, was *meta*-physical, in the Aristotelian sense of being beyond mere physics; 'as long a you seek the moral implications in the physic of sound you fail to find it. You will reason without understanding' (V: 919) . It was the scientists' and the materialists' propensity to 'reason without understanding' which more than anything else was Rousseau's indictment of the philosophy of modernity. Rousseau, the philosopher of the sensible heart, knew that man was a sensitive being (an insight he passed on to the likes of Shelley, Byron, Hölderlin, Mozart and Goethe), and this insight formed the core idea in his political philosophy. Politics (as the science of what ought to be) was grounded in ethics, and ethics could never be but an academic matter. Philosophical reasoning could not 'understand', in the sense of empathy, what it is like to suffer. Reasoning could be useful, but *only* as a means to an end. The moralist – which is everybody who wants to do good – should *not* be a rationalist, but allow him- or herself to be overwhelmed by emotion. 'You must be moved to move others … you must light a fire in your own heart and carry it on to others' (V: 613). To accomplish this it was necessary 'to make language into song, and make the music into words' (V: 445). Rousseau's position has been summed up by Christopher Kelly as follows: 'whereas Plato [was] interested in taming the power of music and submitting it to reason, Rousseau [was] interested in taking advantage of the untamed power of melody. Perhaps because he regard[ed] social life as unnatural, Rousseau ... turn[ed] on its head the platonic order that gives primacy to reason over feeling' (Kelly 1997: 30). And – as mentioned above – man (as a sensitive being) is distinguished by his ability to express emotions through music, for 'nature itself produces few musical tones. It is only living beings who create them' (V: 421)

Whether Rousseau succeeded as a musician and composer – 'made language into song' – is debatable. But he arguably accomplished the feat of writing poetically about politics – and through his skills as a musician – he *aroused* feelings about injustice, something which few – either before or after – have achieved. He made 'music into words'. And this was politically – or philosophically – important. 'The point is', said Rousseau, that music 'can arouse in our heart the same pulsations as one feels in seeing [our fellow beings]' (V: 861). This was not merely a point of musicology but rather an allusion to those powers of empathy and imagination which lay at the heart of his moral theory. Through arousal of our emotions by music (or words as poetical as melody) man could return to his original purity: 'music was born in the same instance as speech. The very first words uttered were sung' (V: 410). But speech degenerated into rational – and disenchanted – discourse. Neither philosophy, nor science could make the world habitable for man. The arts and the sciences – the burden of an inhumane culture – had undermined man's original compassion. This could not be remedied through mere words. Only sounds, which evoke responses that had once been experienced by other senses and which used man's imagination as a backdrop could save us, as Rousseau explained, 'music acts more intimately on us in exciting by one sense affections similar to those, which could be held by another being' (V: 410). Music held out the promise of re-enchanting the world. The physician had identified the disease – it is time to begin the treatment. As Rousseau wrote when he first entered upon the literary stage:

> I must admit that the evil is not as great as it might have become. Eternal foresight, by placing medical herbs next to the various noxious plants, and the remedy against their injuries into substance of a number of harmful animals, has taught the sovereigns who are its ministers to imitate wisdom. (III: 26)

There is hope – after all!

Notes

1 There are rather few studies on this subject. The avid reader should consult Robert Wokler, *Rousseau on Society, Politics, Music and Language* (New York: Garland, 1987); Michael O'Dea, *Jean-Jacques Rousseau: Music, Illusion, and Desire* (New York: St. Martin's Press, 1995); and Thomas M. Kavanagh, *Writing the Truth. Authority and Desire in Rousseau* (Berkeley, University of California Press, 1987).

2 Rousseau's enmity towards Rameau was not surprising. In 1745 Rousseau had revised Rameau and Voltaire's opera *Les Fêtes de Ramire*, which became a success. Yet Rousseau did not receive credit for the work.

Chronology of Rousseau's life (1712–78)

1712   Born in Geneva in a Protestant family. His mother dies in childbirth.

1722   Rousseau's father, Isaac, is forced to leave Geneva, and Rousseau spends two years in the care of a local minister. His father later remarries and abandons Jean-Jacques.

1727   Rousseau begins work as an apprentice to an engraver and flees the following year. The sixteen-year-old meet Mme de Warrens. With her encouragement he converts to Catholicism. She ensures him a position as a servant for Mme de Vercellis and the Count de Gouvon. Guilty of a petty crime, Rousseau blames the deed on an innocent maid.

1729   Returns to Mme de Warrens, attends a seminary but is – understandably – deemed unfit for priesthood.

1730–32 Spends two years hiking. During the winter months he lives in Neuchatel, where he gives music lessons. He goes to Paris for the first time to seek his fortune as a tutor, but is only offered jobs as a servant. Begins to earn his living from note-copying.

1732–36 Returns to Mme de Warrens. The two become lovers. Begins writing, composing and gives music lessons. Writes *Narcissus*.

1737   Goes to Geneva to claim his maternal inheritance, and travels on to Montpellier. Returns to Mme de Warrens, and finds himself displaced by another toyboy.

1740   Finds work in Lyon as tutor for M. de Mably's children. Unhappy he returns to Mme de Warrens.

1742   Rousseau – driven by *amour propre* – seeks his fortune in the fast lane. He presents a new method for musical notation and becomes acquainted with the famous men of letters.

1743   Looking for support from upper-class women he finds work as a tutor for Mme Dupin. Through Mme de Broglie he finds work as an assistant for the French ambassador to Venice. He feels let down because of his background. Decides to write *Institutions Politique*, which in due course becomes *Du Contrat Social*. Writes *Dissertation sur la musique moderne* and *Les Muses galantes*.

1744–45   He returns to Paris but begins to feel ill at ease with the somewhat superficial life in the Paris salons. He begins a life-long relationship with Thrérèse Levasseur, a cleaning lady, who gives birth to four children (all sent to the foundling home). Also in this year he revises Rameau's and Voltaire's opera *Les Fêtes de Ramire*. It becomes a success but Rousseau receives no credit for the work.

1746–48   Rousseau accompanies the Dupin family. M. de Dupin writes a small book about Montesquieu, and discusses political theory with Rousseau, who develops an interest in the subject.

1749   Rousseau reads an advert in a newspaper asking 'if the re-establishment of the arts and the sciences have contributed to an improvement in the morals of man'. He writes the *Discourse sur les sciences et les arts*, and becomes famous.

1751   The first volume of the *Encyclopedia* is published. Rousseau reveals in a letter why he has abandoned his children.

1752   Rousseau composes *Le Devin du Village* and presents it for the king. He is offered a lifelong pension. He refuses!

1753   He publishes the *Letter on French Music* (written the previous year). He praises Italian music and disparages French music – especially that of Rameau.

1754   He writes the *Discourse sur l'inégalité*, the *Discourse on Political Economy*, returns to Geneva (regains his citizenship) but soon returns to France, where he breaks up with his friends. Begins writing *Essai sur l'origine des langues*.

1756–62   Upon an invitation of Mme d'Epinay, Rousseau retires to a cottage ('L'Ermitage') in the woods of Montmorency, where in the quiet of nature he expected to spend his life. He breaks with Diderot. However, he becomes infatuated with Countess d'Houdetot, and after a scandalous scene he changes his residence to a chateau in the park of the duke of Luxembourg, in Montmorency (1758–62). During this period he writes: *Letter à Voltaire sur la Providence* (1756); *Lettre à d'Alembert* (published in Amsterdam, 1758); *Julie ou la nouvelle Heloïse* (1761); *Du Contrat Social* (published in Amsterdam, 1762); and *Emile ou de l'éducation* (published in Amsterdam, 1762). The last-named work was ordered to be burned by the French parliament and his arrest was demanded. In 1762 Rousseau escapes to Neuchatel, then within the jurisdiction of Prussia. He begins *Le Lévite d'Ephraïm* and *Lettre à Christophe de Beaumond*. He also begins work on *Pygmalion*. He writes an autobiographical note in a letter to Melherbes.

1763–66   Rousseau writes *Lettres écrites de la montagne*, an analysis of the Genevan constitution. In this he advocates the freedom of religion against the Church and police. Rousseau is driven out of his house by an angry mob (September 1765), he returns to the Isle St. Pierre in the Lake of Bienne (where he writes *Projet sur la constitution de la Corse*). But the government of Berne orders him out of its territory, and he accepts the asylum offered to him by David Hume in England (January 1766). He falls out with Hume (driven by an insane sense of being persecuted).

1767–78   He returns to France. Marries Thrérèse Levasseur. After wandering about – under the assumed name of Renou – and depending on friends he is permitted to return to Paris (1770), where he finishes the *Confessions* and other biographical writings, *Rousseau juge de Jean-Jacques (Dialogues)*, as well as his *Considérations sur la gouvernement du Pologne* and *Lettres sur la botanique à Madame Delessert*.

1778   He accepts an invitation to retire to Ermenonville, but dies soon after. Shortly before his death he writes his *Revieries d'un promeneur solitaire*.

1794   His remains are taken from Ermenonville to Parthéon, where his coffin is placed next to Voltaire's.

Bibliography

References to Rousseau's work

All references to Rousseau's works are (unless otherwise stated) to the Pléiade edition of his collected works, the full bibliographical details of which are: Jean-Jacques Rousseau, *Oeuvres complètes* (Gallimard: Bibliothèque de la Pléiade, 1959–95), 5 vols, edited by Bernard Gagnebin and Marcel Raymond. (I have used other references if I found that these translations were better than my own.)

The contents of the 5 Pléiade volumes are:

Vol. I (1959): *Les Confessions* and other autobiographical writings.

Vol. II (1961): *Julie* and other literary texts.

Vol. III (1964): *Du Contrat Social* and other political writings.

Vol. IV (1969): *Émile* and writings on education, morality and botany.

Vol. V (1995): Writings on music, languages, theatre (containing, inter alia, *Lettre à D'Alembert*, *l'Essai sur l'origine des langues* and the *Dictionnaire de musique*.

All references to Rousseau's letters are to *Correspondance complète de Jean-Jacques Rousseau*, edited and compiled by Ralph A. Leigh (Geneva and Oxford: Voltaire Foundation, 1965–), 53 vols.

Rousseau, Jean-Jacques (1835) 'Dialogues', in *Oeuvres Complétes de J.J. Rousseau*, Vol. IV, Paris: Chez Furne.

Other works by Rousseau

Rousseau, Jean-Jacques (1962) 'Projet sur la Constitution pour la Corse', in C.E. Vaughan (ed.), *The Political Writings of Jean-Jacques Rousseau*. Oxford: Basil Blackwell.

Rousseau, Jean-Jacques (1968a) *La Nouvelle Héloïse*. University Park: The Pennsylvania State University Press.

Rousseau, Jean-Jacques (1968b) *The Social Contract*. London: Penguin.

Rousseau, Jean-Jacques (1979a) *Emile or on Education*. London, Penguin.

Rousseau, Jean-Jacques (1979b) *Reveries of the Solitary Walker*. London: Penguin.

Rousseau, Jean-Jacques (1985) *The Government of Poland*. Indianapolis: Hackett Publishing.

Rousseau, Jean-Jacques (1992) *The Confessions*. London: Everyman.

Rousseau, Jean-Jacques (1997) *Revieries du promeneur solitaire*. Bourdeaux: Larousse.

Books about Rousseau's work

Needless to say the literature on Rousseau – a man who hated books – is vast. These texts may prove useful:

De Beer, Gavin (1972) *Jean-Jacques Rousseau and His World*. New York: Putnam's Sons.

Gagnebin, Bernard (ed.) (1962) *La rencontre de Jean-Jacques Rousseau*. Genève: Georg.

Guéhenno, Jean (1948–52) *Jean-Jacques Rousseau*. Paris: Grasset, puis Gallimard, 3 vols.

Howlett, Marc-Vincent (1989) *Jean-Jacques Rousseau: l'homme qui croyait en l'homme*. Paris: Gallimard.

Masters, R. (1968) *The Political Philosophy of Rousseau*. Princeton: Princeton University Press.

Soëtard, Michel (1989) *Jean-Jacques Rousseau*. Genève et Lucerne: Coeckelberghs.

Trousson, Raymond (1988–89) *Jean-Jacques Rousseau*. Paris: Tallandier, 2 vols.

Trousson, Raymond (1993) *Jean-Jacques Rousseau: heurs et malheurs d'une conscience*. Paris: Hachette.

For a further overview of the literature one might consult one of the authoritative bibliographies:

McEachern, Jo-Ann E. (1993) *Bibliography of the Writings of Jean Jacques Rousseau to 1800*. Oxford: Voltaire Foundation.

Sénelier, Jean (1950) *Bibliographie générale des oeuvres de J.-J. Rousseau*. Paris: PUF.

Other works cited

Althusser, L. (1970) 'Sur le Contrat Social (les décalages)', in *Cahiers pour l'analyse*, Vol. 8.

Anderson, B. (1982) *Imagined Communities: Reflections on the Origin and Spread of Nationalism*. Cambridge: Cambridge University Press.

Aquinas, T. (2002) *Political Writings*. Cambridge: Cambridge University Press.

Arendt, H. (1958) *The Origins of Totalitarianism*. New York: Meridan.

Aristotle (1984) *The Politics*. Cambridge: Cambridge University Press.

Baczko, B. (n.d.) *Rousseau: solitude et communauté*. Paris: Mouton.

Barber, B. (1987) 'Totalitarianism', in David Miller (ed.) *The Blackwell Encyclopaedia of Political Theory*. Oxford: Blackwell.

Barber. B. (1988) 'Political Participation and the Creation of Res Publica', in Alan Ritter and Julia C. Bondanella (eds) *Rousseau's Political Writings*. London: Norton.

Barker, E. (1948) 'Introduction', in J-J. Rousseau, *The Social Contract*. New York: Oxford University Press.

Barny, R. (1986) *Rousseau dans la Révolution: le personage de Jean-Jacques et les débuts du culte révolutionnaire (1787–1791)*. Oxford: Voltaire Forundation.

Barry, N. (1995) 'Hume, Smith, and Rousseau on Freedom', in R. Wokler (ed.) *Rousseau and Liberty*. Manchester: Manchester University Press.

Bayle, P. (n.d.) *Continuation de Pensées Diverses*, cxxiv, Vol. III.

Berlin, I. (1953) *The Hedgehog and the Fox*. New York: Weidenfeld & Nicholson.

Berlin, I. (1969) *Four Essays on Liberty*. Oxford: Oxford University Press.

Best, G. (1980) *Humanity in Warfare*. Oxford: Oxford University Press.

Blackburn, R. (1996) *The Electoral System in the United Kingdom*. London: Macmillan.

Bloom, A. (ed.) (1960) *Politics and the Arts. Letter to M. d'Alembert on the Theatre by Jean-Jacques Rousseau*. Glencoe Ill: The Free Press.

Blum, S. (1985) 'Rousseau's Concept of Sistême Musical and the Comparative Study of Tonalities in Nineteenth Century France', *Journal of the American Musicological Society*, Vol. 38.

Brooke, C. (2001) 'Rousseau's Political Philosophy', in P. Riley (ed.) *The Cambridge Campanion to Rousseau*. Cambridge: Cambridge University Press.

Burke, E. (1887) *A Vindication of Natural Society*, in Burke, *The Works of the Hon. Edmund Burke*, Vol. 1. London: John Nommo.

Burke, E. (1902) 'Speech to the Electors in Bristol', in *The Works of Edmund Burke*. London: George Bell and Sons (Bohn Standard Library).

Burke, E., 1986, *Reflections on the Revolution in France*, London, Penguin

Burke, E. (1991) 'Letter to a Member of the French National Assembly', in Isaac Kramnick (ed.) *The Portable Edmund Burke*. London: Penguin.

Byron (1994) *The Works of Byron*. London: Wordsworth Editions.

Cameron, D. (1973) *The Social Thought of Rousseau and Burke*. London: Weidenfeld and Nicholson.

Casanova, G. (1968) *History of My Life*, trans. Willard R. Trask. New York: Harcourt, Brace & World Inc.

Charvet, J. (1974) *The Social Problem in the Philosophy of Rousseau*. Cambridge: Cambridge University Press.

Cobban, A. (1969) *Rousseau and the Modern State*. London: Allen & Unwin.

Cohler, A. (1970) *Rousseau and Nationalism*. New York: Basic Books.

Comte, A. (1854) *Systéme de la philosophie positive*. Paris: N.A., Vol. I.

Cranston, M. (1983) *Jean-Jacques: The Early Life and Work of Jean-Jacques Rousseau, 1712–1754*. New York: Norton.

Cranston, M. (1991) *The Noble Savage: Jean-Jacques Rousseau 1754–1762*. London: Penguin.

Cranston, M. (1997) *The Solitary Self: Jean-Jacques Rousseau in Exile and Adversity*. Chicago: University of Chicago Press.

Crocker, L. (1968) *Rousseau's Social Contract: An Interpretive Essay*. Cleveland: Case Western University Press.

Crocker, L. (1968–73) *Jean-Jacques Rousseau*. New York: Macmillan.

Cronin, T. (1989) *Direct Democracy. The politics of Initiative, Referendum and Recall*. Cambridge MA: Harvard University Press.

Constant, B. (1988) *Political Writings*. Cambridge: Cambridge University Press.

De Beer, G. (1972) *Jean-Jacques Rousseau and his world*. New York: Putnam's Sons.

De Man, P. (1979) *Allegories of reading: figural language in Rousseau, Nietzsche, Rilke, and Proust*. New Haven: Yale University Press.

Dent, N.J.H. (1992) *A Rousseau dictionary*. Oxford: Blackwell.

Derathé, R. (1988) *Jean-Jacques Rousseau et la science politique de son temps*. Paris: J. Vrin.

Descartes, R. (1994) *Discourse de la Méthode*. Notre Dame: University of Notre Dame Press.

Diderot, D. (1765) 'Hobbes', in *Encyclopédie*, Tome viii. Neuchatel: Samuel Faulche.

Diderot, D. (1994–97) *Oeuvres I-V*. Paris: Robert Laffont.

Dicey, A.V. (1910) 'The Referendum and Its Critics', *Quarterly Review*, Vol 10, No. 2.

Dobbek, W. (1949) *J.G. Herders Humanititatsideal als Ausdruck seines Weltbildes und seine Personlickeit*. Frankfurt: Braunschweig.

Durkheim, E. (1918) 'Le Contrat Social de Rousseau', in *Revue de Metaphysique et Morale*, xxv.

Ertman, T. (1997) *The Birth of the Leviathan*. Cambridge: Cambridge University Press.

Eliot, T.S. (1975) 'What is a Classic?', *Selected Prose*. New York: Harcourt.

Fabre, J. (1962) 'Realité et Utopie dans la Pensée de Rousseau', in *Annales de Societé Jean-Jacques Rousseau*, Tome 45.

Fergusson, A. (1767) *An Essay on the History of Civil Society*. Edinburgh: n.p.

Fernon, N. (1997) *Domesticating Passions. Rousseau, Women and Nation*. London: Wesleyan University Press.

Fetcher, I. (1960) *Rousseaus politische Philosophie*. Neuwied: Hermann Luchterhand.

Filmer, R. (1949) *Patriarcha and Other Political Writings of Sir Robert Filmer*. Oxford: Blackwell.

Fortescue J. (1885) *The Governance of England; Otherwise called the Difference between absolute and limited monarchy*. Oxford: Clarendon Press.

Foucault, M. (1996a) 'What is an Author', in P. Rabinow (ed.) *The Foucault Reader*. London: Penguin.

Foucault, M. (1996b) 'Nietzsche, Genealogy and History', in P. Rabinow (ed.) *The Foucault Reader*. London: Penguin.

France, P. (1979) 'Introduction', in J.-J. Rousseau, *Reveries of the Solitary Walker*. London: Penguin.

Fralin. R. (1978) *Rousseau and Representation: A Study of the Development of his Concept of Political Institutions*. New York: Columbia University Press.

Fridén, B. (1998) *Rousseau's Economic Philosophy: Beyond the Marked of the Innocents*. Dortrecht: Kluwer Academic Publishers.

Froese, K. (2001) *Rousseau and Nietzsche. Toward an Aesthetic Morality*. Lexington Books: Oxford.

Fukuyama, F. (1992) *The End of History and the Last Man*. London: Penguin.

Gadamer, H.G. (1960) *Wahrheit und Methode*. Tubingen: Mohr.

Gagnebin B. (ed.) (1962) *La rencontre de Jean-Jacques Rousseau*. Genève: Georg.

Gell, L. (1998) *Aufbruch der Freiheit*. Nicolai: Frankfurt am Main.

Gellner, E. (1983) *Nations and Nationalism*. Oxford: Basil Blackwell.

Gellner, E. (1996) *Nationalism*. London: Phoenix.

Guéhenno, J. (1948–52), *Jean-Jacques Rousseau*. Paris: Grasset, 3 vols.

Goethe, J.W.v. (2001) *Faust. Der Tragödie. Zweiter Teil*. Stuttgart: Reclam.

Gourevitch, V. (ed.) (1997a) *Rousseau: The Discourses and other Early Political Writings*. Cambridge: Cambridge University Press.

Gourevitch, V. (ed.) (1997b) *Rousseau: The Social Contract and other Later Political Writings*. Cambridge: Cambridge University Press.

Gourevitch, V. (1998) 'Recent Work on Rousseau', *Political Theory*, No. 4, August.

Gourevitch, V. (2001), 'The Religious Thought', in P. Riley (ed.), *The Cambridge Companion to Rousseau*. Cambridge: Cambridge University Press.

Greenwald B. and J.E. Stieglitz (1986) 'Externalities in Economies with Imperfect Information and Incomplete Markets', *Quarterly Journal of Economics*, Vol. 101, No. 2.

Grey, J. (1995) *Enlightenment's Wake. Politics and Culture at the Close of the Modern Age*. London: Routledge.

Grey, J. (1998) *Voltaire*. London: Routledge.

Grimsley, R. (1968) *Rousseau and Religious Quest*. Oxford: Oxford University Press.

Grofman B and S.L. Feld (1989), 'Rousseau's General Will: A Condorcetian Perspective', *American Political Science Review*, Vol. 82.

Gutman, R.W. (1999) *Mozart: A Cultural Biography*. London: Secker & Warburg.

Hall, J.A. (1995) 'Introduction', in J. A. Hall (ed.) *The State and the Nation*. Cambridge: Cambridge University Press.

Hamilton, A., J. Madison and J. Jay (1961) *The Federalist Papers*. New York: Mentor.

Hampsher-Monk, I. (1995) 'Rousseau and Totalitarianism – with hindsight', in R. Wokler (ed.), *Rousseau and Liberty*. Manchester: Manchester University Press.

Hampson, N. (1990) *The Enlightenment*. London: Penguin.

Handel, C.W. (1934) *Jean-Jacques Rousseau, Moralist*. Oxford:, Oxford University Press.

Hayek, F.A. (1948) *Individualism and Economic Order*. Chicago: Chicago University Press.

Hayek, F.A. (1960) *The Constitution of Liberty*. London: Routledge.

Hayek, F.A. (1978) *New Essays*. London: Routledge.

Hayman, R. (2000) *Nietzsche*. London: Phoenix.

Hulliung, M. (1994) *The Autocritique of Enlightenment. Rousseau and the Philosophers*. Cambridge, MA: Harvard University Press.

Hulliung, M. (2001) 'Rousseau, Voltaire and the Revenge of Pascal', in P. Riley (ed.), *The Cambridge Companion to Rousseau*. Cambridge: Cambridge University Press.

Helvétius, C.A. (1973) *De L'Esprit*. Paris: Verviers.

Hirschman, N. (2002) 'Rousseau's Republican Romance', Review Article, in *Political Theory*, Vol. 30, No. 1.

Hobbes, T. (1973) *Leviathan*. London: Everyman.

Hobbes, T. (1998) *On the Citizen*. Cambridge: Cambridge University Press.

Hobsbawm, E. (1990) *Nations and Nationalism since 1780*. Cambridge: Cambridge University Press.

Höffding, H. (1910) *Rousseau und seine Philosophie*. Stuttgart: Frommann.

Holmsten, G. (1972) *Jean-Jacques Rousseau*. Hamburg: Rowohlt.

Howlett, M.-V. (1989) *Jean-Jacques Rousseau: l'homme qui croyait en l'homme*. Paris: Gallimard.

Hugo, V. (1995) *Les Misérables*. Paris: Gallimard.

Hume, D. (1932) *The Letters of David Hume*, edited by J.Y.L. Greig. Oxford: Clarendon Press.

Hume, D. (1985) *Essays, Moral, Political and Literary*. Indianapolis: Liberty Fund.

Johnston, S. (2002) 'Rousseau's Refusal', *Political Theory*, December, Vol. 30, No. 6.

Jones, J.F. (1991) *Rousseau's Dialogues: An Interpretive Essay*. Genève: Droz.

Jouvenel, B.D (1965) 'Rousseau, évolutioniste, pessimiste', in *Rousseau et la Philosophie classique*. Paris: Presses Universitaires de France.

Kant, I. (1868) *Fragmente aus dem Nachlässe*, in *Kants Sämtliche Werke*, Vol. VIII. Leipzig: Leopold Voss.

Kavanagh, T.M. (1987) *Writing the Truth: Authority and Desire in Rousseau*. Berkeley: University of California Press.

Kavanagh, T.M. (2001) 'Rousseau's The Levite of Ephrahim', in P. Riley (ed.), *The Cambridge Campanion to Rousseau*. Cambridge: Cambridge University Press.

Keats, J. (1994) *Poems*. London: Everyman.

Keegan, J. (1993) *A History of Warfare*. London: Hutchinson.

Kedouri, E. (1960) *Nationalism*. Oxford: Basil Blackwell.

Kendal, W. (1985) 'Introduction', in J.-J. Rousseau, *The Government of Poland*. New York: Hackett Publishing.

Kelly, C. (1987) *Rousseau's Exemplary Life: The Confessions as Political Philosophy*. London: Cornell University Press.

Kelly, C. (1997) 'Rousseau and the Case Against (and for) the Arts', in C. Orwin and N. Tarcov (eds) *The Legacy of Rousseau*. Chicago: University of Chicago Press.

Klein, J. (2002) *The Natural. The Misunderstood Presidency of Bill Clinton*. New York: Coronet Books.

Launay, M. (1963) 'La societé francaise d'apres le Correspondance de Jean-Jacques Rousseau', in *Societé des Etudes Robbespierristes; Jean-Jacques Rousseau*. Paris: GAP.

Launay, M. (1989) *Jean-Jacques Rousseau écrivain politique: 1712–1762*. Paris et Genève: Slatkine.

Leigh, R.A. (1964) 'Liberté et autorité dans le Contrat Social', in *Jean-Jacques Rousseau et son oeuvre*. Paris: Klinckseik.

Leigh, R.A. (ed.) (1982) *Rousseau After Two Hundred Years*. Cambridge: Cambridge University Press.

Levine, A. (1993) *The General Will: Rousseau, Marx, Communism*. Cambridge:

Cambridge University Press.

Levmore, S. (1992) 'Bicameralism: When are Two Decisions Better than One?', *International Review of Law and Economics*, Vol. 12, No. 2.

Levy (1971) *The Early History of Rome*, edited by R.M. Oglive. New York: Penguin.

MacIntyre, A. (1981) *After Virtue*. London: Duckworth.

Machiavelli, M (1994) 'The Discourses', in *Selected Political Writings*. Indianapolis: Hackett Publishing.

Marsilius of Padua (1951) *The Defensor of the Peace*. New York: Harper-Torch Books.

Marx, K. (1962) 'Thesen über Feuerbach', in K. Marx and F. Engels, *Werke*. Berlin: Dietz, Vol. 3.

Marx, K. (1962) 'Das Kapital', in K. Marx and F. Engels, *Werke*. Berlin: Dietz, Vol. 23.

Marx, K. (1977) *Karl Marx: Selected Writings*, edited by David McLellan. Oxford: Oxford University Press.

Marx, K. (1978) *The Marx-Engels Reader*, edited by Robert Tucker. New York: W.W. Norton.

Masters, R. (1968) *The Political Philosophy of Rousseau*. Princeton: Princeton University Press.

May, G. (2002) 'Rousseau, Cultural Critic', in Susan Dunn (ed.) *The Social Contract and the First and Second Discourses*. New Haven: Yale University Press.

McClelland, J.S. (1996) *A History of Western Political Philosophy*. London: Routledge.

McCormick, J.P. (2001) 'Machiavellian Democracy: Controlling Elites with Ferocious Populism', *American Political Science Review*, Vol. 95, June.

Macpherson, C.B. (1962) *The Political Theory of Possesive Individualism. Hobbes to Locke*. Oxford: Oxford University Press.

Melzer, A.M. (1990) *The Natural Goodness of Man*. Chicago: University of Chicago Press.

Mercier, L.-S. (1791) *De J.-J. Rousseau consideré comme l'un des premiers auteurs de la revolution*. Paris: Buisson, 2 vols.

Miller, D. (1995) *On Nationality*. Oxford: Oxford University Press.

Miller, J. (1984) *Rousseau: Dreamer of Democracy*. New Haven: Yale University Press.

Montesquieu, C. (1968) *Considérations sur les causes de la grandeur de Romains et de leur decadence*. Madrid: Garmier-Flammaignon.

Montesquieu, C. (1989) *The Spirit of the Laws*. Cambridge: Cambridge University Press.

Mueller, D. (1996) *Constitutional Democracy*. Oxford: Oxford University Press.

Nietzsche, F. (1883) *Also Sprach Zaratustra. Ein Buch für alle und keinen*. Chemnitz: Verlag von Ernst Schmeitzner.

Nietzsche, F. (1969) *Ecce Homo*, in F. Nietzsche, *Kritische Gesamtaufgabe*. Berlin: Walter de Gruyter.

Nozick, R. (1973) *Anarchy, State and Utopia*. Oxford: Blackwell.

Oakeshott, M. (1991) *Rationalism in Politics and Other Essays*. Indianapolis: Liberty Fund.

O'Dea, M. (1995) *Jean-Jacques Rousseau: music, illusion, and desire*. New York: St. Martin's Press.

O'Brien, C.C. (2002) 'Rousseau, Robespierre, and the French Revolution', in S. Dunn (ed.) *The Social Contract and the First Discourses*. New Haven: Yale University Press.

O'Hagan, T. (1999) *Rousseau*. London: Routledge.

O Leary B. (1998) 'Ernest Gellner's Diagnoses of Nationalism: A Critical Appraisal', in J. A. Hall (ed.), *The State and the Nation*. Cambridge: Cambridge University Press.

Osborn, Annie Marion (1940) *Rousseau and Burke: A Study of the Idea of Liberty in Eighteenth Century Political Thought*. Oxford: Oxford University Press.

Pateman, C. (1970) *Participation and Democratic Theory*. Cambridge: Cambridge University Press.

Plato (1953) *The Dialogues of Plato*, Vol. IV, edited by B. Jowett. Oxford: Clarendon.

Plato (1974) *The Laws*, edited by T. Saunders. London: Penguin.

Plato (1975) *The Republic*. London: Penguin.

Popper, K. (1945) *The Open Society and Its Enemies II*. London: Routledge.

Popper, K. (1992) *Unended Quest*. London: Routledge.

Putnam, R. (2000) *Bowling Alone. The Collapse and Revival of American Community*. New York: Simon and Schuster.

Putterman, E. (1999) 'Rousseau's Conception of Property', *History of Political Thought*, Vol. 20, No. 3.

Putterman, E. (2001) 'Realism and Reform in Rousseau's Constitutional projects for Poland and Corsica', *Political Studies*, Vol. 49.

Qvortrup, M. (2002) *A Comparative Study of Referendums. Government by the People*. Manchester: Manchester University Press.

Rawls, J. (1971) *A Theory of Justice*. Oxford: Oxford University Press.

Richter, M. (1995) 'Rousseau and Tocqueville on Democratic Legitimacy and Illegitimacy', in R. Wokler (ed.) *Rousseau and Liberty*. Manchester: Manchester University Press.

Riker, W. (1982) *Liberalism against Populism*. Prospect Heights, IL: Waveland Inc. Press.

Riley P. (ed.) (2001a) *The Cambridge Companion to Rousseau*. Cambridge: Cambridge University Press.

Riley, P. (2001b) 'Introduction: The Life and Works of Jean-Jacques Rousseau (1712–1778)', in P. Riley (ed.) *The Cambridge Companion to Rousseau*. Cambridge: Cambridge University Press.

Schoppenhauer, A. (1958) *The World as Will and Representation Vol. II*. Toronto: Dover.

Shklar, J. (1969) *Men and Citizens. A Study of Rousseau's Social Theory*. Cambridge, Cambridge University Press.

Shklar, J. (1988) 'Jean-Jacques Rousseau and Equality', in A. Ritter and J.C.

Bondanella (eds) *Rousseau's Political Writings*. London: Norton.

Skinner, Q. (1969) 'Meaning and Understanding in the History of the Ideas', *History and Theory*, Vol. 8, No. 1.

Smith, A. (1937) *An Inquiry into the Nature and Causes of the Wealth of Nations*. New York: Random House.

Smith, A. (1994) *National Identity*. London: Penguin.

Soëtard, M. (1989) *Jean-Jacques Rousseau*. Genève et Lucerne: Coeckelberghs.

Spurlin, P.M. (1969) *Rousseau in America*. Alabama: Huntsville.

Starobinski J. (1957) *Jean-Jacques Rousseau: la transparence et l'obstacle*. Paris: Plon, translated as *Transparency and obstruction*, trans. Arthur Goldhammer. Chicago: Chicago University Press [1988].

Starobinsky, J. (1988) 'The Political Philosophy of Jean-Jacques Rousseau', in A. Ritter and J.C. Bondanella (eds) *Rousseau's Political Writings*. London: Norton.

Stiebing, W.T. (1994) *Uncovering the Past. A History of Archaeology*. Oxford: Oxford University Press.

Strong, T. (1994) *Jean-Jacques Rousseau: The Politics of the Ordinary*. London: SAGE Publications.

Swenson, J. (1999) *On Jean-Jacques Rousseau: Considered As One of the First Authors of the Revolution*. Palo Alto: Stanford University Press.

Sydney, A. (1996) *Discourses Concerning Government*. Indianapolis: Liberty Fund.

Talmon, J.L. (1952) *The Origins of Totalitarianism*. London: Secker and Warburg.

Taylor, L. (1990) *Roman Voting Assemblies*. Ann Arbor: University of Michigan Press.

Thompson, D. (1976) *John Stuart Mill and Representative Government*. Princeton: Princeton University Press.

Tocqueville, A. de (1945) *Democracy in America 1–11*. New York: Vintage.

Trousson, R. (1993) *Jean-Jacques Rousseau: heurs et malheurs d'une conscience*. Paris: Hachette.

Trachtenberg, Z. (1993) *Making Citizens. Rousseau's Political Theory of Culture*. New York: Routledge.

Vaughan, C.E. (1962) *The Political Writings of Jean-Jacques Rousseau*. Oxford: Basil Blackwell.

Velkley, R.L. (2002) *Being After Rousseau. Philosophy and Culture in Question*. Chicago: University of Chicago Press.

Vile, M.J.C. (1998) *Constitutionalism and the Separation of Powers*. Indianapolis: Liberty Fund.

Virolli, M. (1988) *Jean-Jacques Rousseau and the Well-Ordered Society*. Cambridge: Cambridge University Press.

Voltaire, J.M. de (n.d.) 'Dictionaire Philosophique', in *Oeuvress Philosophique de Voltaire*. Paris: Hachette, Vol. XVIII.

Voltaire, J.M. de (1973) *Selected Letters of Voltaire*. New York: New York University Press.

Volpe G.D. (1970) 'The Marxist Critique of Rousseau', *New Left Review*, Vol. 59.

Waltz, K. (1959) *Man, The State, and War*. New York: Columbia University Press.

Weber, M. (1997) 'Science as Vocation', in H.H. Gerth and C. Wright-Mills (eds) *From Max Weber. Essays in Sociology*. Routledge: London.

Weil, Eric (1952) 'Rousseau et sa politique', *Critique*, Vol. 56, No. 1.

Whitman, W. (1975) *The Complete Poems*. London: Penguin.

Wingrove, E.R. (2000) *Rousseau's Republican Romance*. Princeton: Princeton University Press.

Wittgenstein, L. (1984a) *Tractatus Logico-Philosophicus*, in L. Wittgenstein, *Gesamtaufgabe*, Vol. 1. Frankfurt am Main: Suhrkamp.

Wittgenstein, L. (1984b) *Philosophische Untersuchungen*, in L. Wittgenstein, *Gesamtausgabe*, Vol. 1. Frankfurt am Main: Suhrkamp.

Wokler, R. (1987) *Rousseau on Society, Politics, Music and Language*. New York: Garland.

Wokler, R. (ed.) (1995a) *Rousseau and Liberty*. Manchester: Manchester University Press.

Wokler, R. (1995b) *Rousseau*. Oxford: Oxford University Press.

Wokler, R. (2001) *Rousseau. A Very Short Introduction*. Oxford: Oxford University Press.

Woolhouse, R.S. (1971) *Locke's Philosophy of Science and Knowledge*. Oxford: Blackwell.

World Bank (2002) 'Can we Discern the Effect of Globalisation on Income Distribution', *World Bank Research Policy Paper*, No. 2876.

Dixi et salavi animam meam[1]

---

[1] I have spoken and relieved my soul.

Index